Rum-Runners & Mobsters

Prohibition's 100th Anniversary in Newfoundland

© 2017, Jack Fitzgerald

 Canada Council Conseil des Arts
for the Arts du Canada

Canada

Newfoundland
Labrador

We gratefully acknowledge the financial support of the Canada Council for the Arts,
the Government of Canada through the Canada Book Fund (CBF),
and the Government of Newfoundland and Labrador through the Department
of Tourism, Culture and Recreation for our publishing program.

Printed on acid-free paper
Cover Design Maurice Fitzgerald
Layout by Fenton Fortune

Published by
Creative Publishers
an imprint of CREATIVE BOOK PUBLISHING
a Transcontinental Inc. associated company
P.O. Box 8660, Stn. A
St. John's, Newfoundland and Labrador A1B 3T7

Printed in Canada by: Marquis

Library and Archives Canada Cataloguing in Publication

Fitzgerald, Jack, 1943-, author
        Rum-runners and mobsters : prohibition's 100th anniversary
in Newfoundland / Jack Fitzgerald.

Includes bibliographical references.
ISBN 978-1-77103-098-4 (softcover)

        1. Prohibition--Newfoundland and Labrador--History.
2. Smuggling--Newfoundland and Labrador--History. 3. Organized
crime--Newfoundland and Labrador--History. 4. Newfoundland and
Labrador--History. I. Title.

HV5091.C3F58 2017   364.13309718   C2016-907446-3

Rum-Runners & Mobsters

Prohibition's 100th Anniversary in Newfoundland

Jack Fitzgerald

St. John's, Newfoundland and Labrador, 2017

Dedication

This book is dedicated
to the late *Mike Critch*,
longtime friend and mentor, who was
awarded a lifetime achievement award
from the Canadian Association of Radio
and Television Broadcasting

Table of Contents

Chapter 1

Mobsters Hide Behind Newfoundland Flag

There is nothing among ship movement records in Newfoundland during the American Prohibition years to suggest something reprehensible and devious was going on in the colony.

Not a thing to cause anyone to suspect that crime syndicates in the United States and Canada, or even the Newfoundland people, knew what was going on and going on with the approval of Newfoundland's government, which accommodated the scheme from the beginning.

Not a thing to indicate that some Newfoundland merchants were up to their arses in the scheme to the extent of direct involvement.

Beneath the surface, beyond the daily record of Newfoundland-registered vessels, was a cleverly developed plan to use Newfoundland and its laws for the benefit of gangsters, rum-runners and smugglers. This was a scheme that enabled fortunes to be made, despite the collateral damage of ruined lives, violence and death.

The significance of the role Newfoundland played once the smugglers mastered its customs laws was described by Jean Pierre Andrieux, a St. Pierre historian and expert on the Prohibition era. He wrote:

> Contrary to popular belief, St. John's was a very active base for rum-running during [American] Prohibition.

There were transhipments of alcohol taking place through the Furness Withy wharf in St. John's. Large bonded stocks were coming in from England and Canada and they were held in large warehouses. You could get a clearance for the high seas from St. John's which was legal but in many cases the liquor was actually going to the south coast for shipment to the United States.

The information supplied, either directly or indirectly, to criminal organizations by Newfoundland's Justice Department reads like a handbook on how to by-pass American and Canadian Prohibition laws.

American Mobsters Took Notice of Newfoundland

Organized crime developed more than a passing interest in Newfoundland's customs law, which they were correctly led to believe left the field of rum-running and smuggling wide open during the American Prohibition years. Without any confirmation at this point, they could only dream of the opportunities that would open to them if reports were true. Perhaps Newfoundland might even rival St. Pierre as a convenient transhipment port.

One could only imagine fellows like Capone, Dutch Shultz and the Torrio brothers consulting their legal advisers to see if this could be a "One up for the gang." Little doubt, it played no small role in the flurry of written enquires from sources in New York, Boston and even Montreal which began arriving on the desk of Newfoundland's minister of justice.

Top justice officials, to the chagrin of Britain, began providing assurances which were of primary interest to the extensive rum-running operations already making millions by supplying liquor, illegally, to the U.S. market (then in the middle of suffering its "long thirst.") The official responses brought about a massive shift in how the rum-smuggling business was operated.

The first disclosure from Newfoundland justice officials revealed that when Newfoundland Prohibition ended, bonded warehouses in Newfoundland remained open and operated freely in the transhipment of alcohol.

Criminal organizations in the United States, which took over the delivery and distribution of imported liquor during Prohibition, depended on foreign ships to deliver the illegal cargoes to just outside the American twelve-mile limit where, at pre-determined positions along the coast from New York to Boston (the notorious "Rum Row"), American hoods would accept delivery.

Another plus for the bad guys came after learning that the United Distillers of Montreal asked Justice Minister W.J. Higgins, "...if rum [could] be shipped to your city and then exported from there in bond?" His reply, on July 7, 1926, confirmed this was the case but duty was payable upon entry at twelve-and-a-half-cents a gallon.

Britain and U.S. Upset with Newfoundland

When it became known that Britain and the United States had signed a pact to combat the rum-running operations on the Atlantic coast, criminals grew concerned. However, their anxiety was relieved when justice officials, to the great displeasure of England and the United States, made it clear that Newfoundland had no intentions of either returning to Prohibition or aiding in the crackdown on rum-runners. If this point was not made clear enough the Justice Department further clarified, "It would seem that goods in transit and in bond are not 'imported,' and therefore, from the point of view of the said Act are not in the Colony and could be shipped."[1] Also excluded, were wines imported into the country to be

1 Hunter, Mark. *The Cloak of the Newfoundland Registry for American Rumrunning. 1924-1934.*

matured and later exported. A rum-running vessel with Newfoundland registry, if stopped, could justify carrying a liquor cargo by claiming it was in transit or for the crews use. Bon voyage mates!

Newfoundland Politicians Helpful to Rum-runners

The advantage to rum-runners in using St. John's as a transhipment port for liquor was emphasized by the Minister of Justice, William Higgins, who pointed out to those enquiring that the only requirement to be met was the payment of duty upon entry. This was an insignificant cost for the gangsters setting up the Prohibition smuggling operation to supply liquor to the vast American market.

An additional item to the criminals "to do list" was to get the Newfoundland government to clarify its custom laws regarding required documented evidence. The official noted that its customs officers were not required to demand or request any evidence to confirm neither the destination nor arrival of cargo. It was a simple case of just pay the duty then full speed ahead! Damn the torpedoes!

Officials even leaked out intelligence information it received from Britain. One justice record noted, "We can't enforce the laws anywhere. We don't have enough police and magistrates." That news must have turned heads in Chicago and New York. Little wonder that Capone, the Torrio brothers and Legs Diamond had to visit St. John's to see for themselves.

They were probably overjoyed to learn that St. John's, Newfoundland's capital city, could boast of only one inspector of customs, one inspector of preventative service, a clerk and surveyor of shipping, one registrar of shipping and one customs office.[2] With only one enforcement officer, factoring in tea breaks and lunch hours, and at least eighty-one rum-

2 Ibid

4

running vessels regularly using this port, one could imagine how intimidated visiting mob members must have felt.

In his book, *Politics in Newfoundland*, S.J.R. Noel made an observation that applied to Newfoundland during its own Prohibition, 1917-1924, as well as the American Prohibition, 1920-1933. He noted:

> Unenforceable laws are notorious causes of political corruption, especially where fortunes are to be made by their unhindered evasion. In Newfoundland, as in some microcosm of America, Prohibition became a classic case at the same time demonstrating more clearly than ever the weaknesses of a public service based on 'spoils.' Poorly paid and insecure, officials, politicians with an eye to the 'rewards of office' and those who had influence with politicians, suddenly found themselves exposed to, or able to find, temptations on a scale previously unimaginable. And the richer the rewards the more deeply entrenched and resistant to reform the system itself became.[3]

Yet, this alone did not lead to the sudden outbreak on the scene of Newfoundland's involvement in the Atlantic coast smuggling and rum-running operations. That began when the gangsters formulated their plan to create a fleet of Newfoundland-registered ships by changing the port of registry of their own vessels, and adding Newfoundlanders to their crews, to facilitate the smuggling of liquor into the United States.

Smuggling liquor along Rum Row, while using St. Pierre and Newfoundland, evolved into an efficiently organized, well-financed and structured conspiracy. The police, Coast Guard and various commissions set up to investigate the

3 Noel, S.J.R. *Politics in Newfoundland.* University of Toronto Press, 1971. p132.

operation were frequently obstructed from detecting the top people in the organization.

One Newfoundland merchant claimed to own a ship which was registered in Nova Scotia under another man's name. This appears to have been a front for an American interest. Very few of the rum-runners registered as Newfoundland vessels were actually owned by Newfoundlanders. In several cases, Newfoundland owners had leased their vessels to criminal syndicates and their associates in the United States.

This strategy came at an opportune time for the American mobs. The ships that were not American-registered that participated in the huge rum-running business relied mostly on St. Pierre to get their contraband into the United States. However, when the lines of smuggling across the Canadian border were plugged, the result was increased coastal rum-running along Rum Row. The warehouses in St. Pierre were almost continually filled and with their ships now flying under the Newfoundland flag, they were able to store contraband at warehouses in St. John's.

Many Newfoundland fishermen and fishing captains turned to rum-running, and their expertise in sailing on the North Atlantic was a definite asset. There was certainly plenty of opportunity in the trade for those willing to participate. However, rum-running was not without its dangers. In addition to having to evade capture by the American Coast Guard patrols, they were constantly on the lookout for gangsters out to hijack their cargoes.

During American Prohibition over 100,000 people were involved in moonshining, bootlegging and rum-running, all of which, in the United States, were primarily the domain of mobsters. Criminal syndicates in several Canadian provinces were connected with the Americans and had tentacles in St. Pierre and Newfoundland. Criminal groups outside the United States specialized in getting liquor supplies into the United States, where incredible fortunes were being made. These factors contributed to the importance of Newfoundland and St. Pierre to those willing to risk arrest and imprisonment to cash in on the profits.

To meet the expansion on the Atlantic coast, the United States had increased its Coast Guard's presence there. Naval author C.W. Hunt revealed:

> One result was a dramatic increase in smuggling vessels seized on the seaboard. In 1929, the coast guard seized 2,571 vessels, and in 1930, 2,441 vessels, but in 1931 the number climbed to 2919, a 20 percent increase. This was the peak year for the coast guard.[4]

Mark Hunter, historian and authority on the Prohibition era, concluded from his extensive research that, "The Newfoundland government was clearly aware of the benefits it received from the rum-running business."[5]

St. John's and St. Pierre–the Mob's Jewels in the Atlantic

After Prohibition ended in Newfoundland in April 1924, St.John's quickly developed into a gangsters paradise, similar to St. Pierre but with much less notoriety, thanks to a key loophole in Newfoundland laws. Jean Pierre Andrieux, revealed the extent of St. Pierre's similar role during American Prohibition. He explained:

> There were 80 boats waiting in St. Pierre all the time for carriage of this liquor to the 12-mile limit off the United States coast. The Canadian distilleries were shipping their production to the island where it was stored in large concrete warehouses. This operation went through 300,000 cases of alcohol a month.

4 Hunter, C.W. *Booze, Boats and Billions.*
5 Ibid

7

He also disclosed Montreal's role in the Atlantic gangster operations into the United States and Canada. Andrieux noted that criminals met with the distillery owners to make their deals. He explained:

> American syndicates that were buying the alcohol would come up with suitcases of money to the mezzanine of the Mount Royal Hotel. Once paid for, there would be a telegram sent to the distillery's subsidiary in St. Pierre saying to please prepare for so-and-so such and such a boat.

St. Pierre's merchants acted as liquor brokers and charged warehousing fees to store alcohol temporarily. Smugglers were able to land contraband cargoes in St. Pierre and after receiving a stamped document verifying the cargo had landed in that country, could move to the next step in getting the booze past the U.S. Coast Guard and American customs. Canadians were able to ship cargoes this way and then return them to Canada for illegal distribution.

By the late 1920s, large foreign companies, mainly distilleries, dominated the St. Pierre rum trade. The work to prepare the order involved repackaging the liquor from wooden cases into jute sacks with straw covers to reduce noise. It was then loaded aboard ships for transportation to those who would complete the last stage of the activity, smuggling it past American customs. This was achieved by transferring the liquor to American smuggling ships near the twelve-mile limit[6] on dark moonless nights. Although there were no radars in that era, there was a big risk due to the patrols of American Coast Guard clippers. Throughout these activities, St. Pierre was not breaking any laws because it did not have Prohibition. However, the end of the liquor drought in Newfoundland was

6 During American Prohibition the three-mile limit was extended to a twelve-mile limit.

about to add another pearl in the North Atlantic for organized crime. Newfoundland was ready and willing to fill that role

Prohibition Ends for Newfoundland but not Rum-running

By 1924, people realized that instead of curing the social ills of the country, Prohibition had added to them. As a result, on August 12, 1924, the Newfoundland Prohibition Act of 1917 was terminated. However, this opened the door, for those so inclined, in another direction. Both merchants and fishermen availed of the opportunities created by Prohibition in the United States, and a few Canadian provinces, and some made fortunes.

The full extent of that involvement has remained well hidden over the past half century. It is a part of Newfoundland history that will raise many eyebrows. The criminal activity related to Prohibition did not end when the Act was repealed. Criminals profiting from Prohibition in Newfoundland were already very much aware of the immense financial benefits of smuggling contraband liquor into the United States, which was still under Prohibition.

Prohibition in United States began in 1920, and it created illegal and legal opportunities for fortunes to be made. St. Pierre, off Newfoundland's south coast, did not have Prohibition enacted, which is why it played such a major role for the rum-running industry. When Prohibition ended in Newfoundland the country became as important to American gangsters and independent rum-runners as St. Pierre.

Prohibition Years Differed Province to Province

In the United States, Prohibition operated from 1920-1933. In Canada, provinces held jurisdiction so that by 1901, Prince Edward Island was already dry. Manitoba, Nova Scotia, Alberta and Ontario repealed Prohibition in 1916.

Saskatchewan, New Brunswick and British Columbia enacted Prohibition in 1917. The Yukon and Quebec banned liquor sales in 1918 and 1919.

Prohibition ended in New Brunswick in 1927, in Nova Scotia in 1930 and in Prince Edward Island in 1948. Unlike Newfoundland, they were prevented from becoming transhipment ports. Newfoundland's Prohibition ran from 1917-1924, while in St. Pierre Prohibition was never enacted. The variance in Canadian dates for Prohibition was due the Privy Council's decision, 1896-1901. That decision deemed the handling of liquor to be a shared responsibility under which Ottawa could regulate the manufacturing and interprovincial distribution of liquor, while the provinces held responsibility over the control of sales. The alcohol content permitted by federal law was set at 2.5 percent and alcohol consumption was permitted for use in the home.

The distillation and brewing of alcohol beverages, of any strength, for export was permitted. Bootleggers and moonshiners were at work in Canada at this time and were doing good business smuggling Canadian-produced liquor and shipping it to St. Pierre and Newfoundland, where it was then smuggled into the United States and the parts of Canada where Prohibition was being enforced. In Canada, after January 1920, alcohol exports could be made to the United States providing export duties were paid. Exports elsewhere were not taxed. This provided a valuable loophole for Canadians.

In 1926-1927, two investigations, one conducted by a Canadian parliamentary committee and the second by the Royal Commission, gathered evidence connecting a Newfoundland business to a rum-running scheme initiated in Quebec to evade customs and deliver, illegally, cargoes of contraband liquor.

The Canadian firm targeted by investigators was Dominion Distilleries of Lachine, Quebec, opposite Montreal. Dominion Distilleries had succeeded the St. Pierre firm of W.J. George Ltd. as liquor agents. Dominion purchased liquor from the Hiram Walker Distillery. The documents seized from the Hiram Walker Distillers told the story. They shipped liquor to six firms in the Atlantic area, all of which had a connection to W.J. George Ltd. These included a firm in St. John's and another in St. Pierre. The documents showed that these sales were all charged to W.J. George Ltd. but ended up in the hands of Dominion Distilleries. The investigations did not implicate Hiram Walker. However, they gathered valuable evidence to implicate the Newfoundland government and businessmen.

During the Prohibition years in Newfoundland, Newfoundland had its own smuggling operations which were not as large or as well-organized as the one that emerged after the repeal of Prohibition. Journalist, John Calver, in an article published in *Newfoundland Lifestyles* noted that Newfoundland rum-runners, during its Prohibition era, sailed to Demerara, British Guyana, and loaded their schooners with rum, which locally became famous as Screech. This rum was smuggled and sold to bootleggers in the little villages along Newfoundland's coast. Distribution was later expanded into the Maritime Provinces and even Quebec.[7]

The Smugglers Plan to Change the Flag of Registry

When Prohibition ended in Newfoundland its politicians were not mistaken in believing that the loopholes in its Customs Act could financially benefit Newfoundland – legal or not! There were many enquiries from the United States and Canada regarding its custom laws and Newfoundland officials were more than happy to cooperate. Once the syndicates had confirmed claims of loopholes in these laws, and that the

7 Calver, John. *Rumrunning in the Good Old Days.* p46. CNS.

country was willing to turn a blind-eye to smugglers, they recognized the benefit of having Newfoundland-registered ships. This information set wheels in motion among those wanting to supply the American booze market and the gangsters in the United States, who were seizing control of its distribution.

According to journalist Leo Moakler:

> St. John's at this time became a rum-runner's haven by virtue of an Act passed in the House of Assembly in 1898 and never revoked. It enabled the rumrunners to store their contraband liquor in a bonded warehouse in the city and withdraw quantities as required. This loophole was taken advantage of to such an extent that the Auditor General openly accused the Newfoundland government of being in the liquor business.[8]

St. John's Emerges as a Key Rum-running Port

After studying the regular and secret dispatches between London, St. John's and Washington, intelligence lists of suspect vessels, vessels' crew agreements and data from the Atlantic Canada Shipping Project, author Mark Hunter concluded, "The nature of Newfoundland's government and economy was such that during the 1920s the colony provided a safe haven for rumrunners."[9]

When Britain and the United States signed an anti-liquor smuggling pact in 1924, they had hoped to obtain support from St. Pierre and Newfoundland. France refused outright while Newfoundland angered Britain by refusing to cooperate. Perhaps the fact that many of the Newfoundland politicians and

---

8 On one hand, there was a total ban on liquor for its own citizens; while on the other hand, the government was cooperating with lawbreakers to supply the citizens of the United States.

9 Hunter, Mark. "Prohibition" - Newfoundland and Labrador Studies Vol. 21 (2006) p46

businessmen were benefiting or participating in rum-running operations into the United States was a powerful influence. John Bennett, the major shareholder in the Bennett Brewing Company, was a member of the Conservative administration that removed Prohibition. This move helped his company avoid bankruptcy and placed it on the road to prosperity.

Newfoundland's role in the criminal activity surrounding the American era of Prohibition came about when well-informed rum-runners and gangsters saw the benefit of hiding the ownership of their vessels under the registry of a jurisdiction that offered a transhipment port, storage warehouses and had practically no ability to enforce customs laws. In addition, there was no doubt, judging by the signals given officially in Newfoundland, that the colony had interest in interfering. Some Newfoundland politicians and merchants even went as far as to become participants in the grand scheme.

Like St. Pierre, Newfoundland became, to the chagrin of Britain and the United States, a transhipment point for liquor. American gangsters and others benefitting from the smuggling of liquor became aware and eager to use the situation to its maximum advantage.

Prohibition in the United States was introduced on January 16, 1920, under the Eighteenth Amendment of the United States Constitution and the Volstead Act, which defined alcoholic drinks by volume, as any beverage with more than 0.5 percent alcohol. The amendment banned the import and export of alcohol and its manufacture and consumption within American territory. Prohibition lasted for thirteen years, during which time the only access Americans had to alcohol was through it being smuggled into the country from St. Pierre, Newfoundland and Canada.

Newfoundland's Unknown Rum-running Fleet

Armed with the knowledge that having a ship registered in Newfoundland would be beneficial to the smuggling operation going on along the Atlantic coast, smugglers developed a sort of "Rum-runners Navy." Eighty-one vessels switched registry to Newfoundland and many of them employed Newfoundland crews. The registered owners were not all actual owners of the vessels. Several Newfoundland merchants fronted for the real owners.[10]

By the time the transfer of registry was completed, St. John's was the top port of registry for suspected rum-runners. Most of the transfers were carried out by allegedly Canadian owners. However, the *I'm Alone*, with a Newfoundland war hero as captain, was registered to the I'm Alone Shipping Company of Lunenburg which according to Mark Hunter was, "...fronting for a consortium of American bootleggers." The remarkable story of the vessel, *I'm Alone*, built in Lunenburg specifically for rum-running is told in a later chapter.

Another Newfoundland-registered, but Nova Scotia-owned, rum-runner, the *Casanova*, was equipped with sophisticated detection equipment, which included a radio and smoke screen equipment. This was useful when evading Coast Guard cutters along Rum Row.

Captain William Basil Moriarity, who is mentioned in British-American intelligence as a notorious bootlegger, was the real owner of the *Casanova* which was registered to a St. John's-owned company. Moriarity operated multiple rum-runners out of St. Pierre. John McLeod, a mate on one of Moriarity's ships, was connected with American gangsters and wanted in the United States on rum-running charges. While on the Newfoundland-registered ship he used the alias John Davis. These confidential intelligence reports were shared with the Newfoundland government, which turned a blind eye to them.

10 1bid

Commission of Government More Honest

Newfoundland underwent a reversal of policy towards rum-runners when Commission of Government replaced Responsible government. The commission confirmed that large shipments of liquor were moved from bonded warehouses in St. John's to Bermuda. At least that is the destination shown on the stamped documents carried by the vessels.

Somewhere along the route there would be a short diversion to Rum Row. If per chance the ship was stopped outside the twelve-mile limit, the certificate of destination from St. John's was its protection against arrest.

Unlike Responsible government, the Commission of Government shared its intelligence information with the American consulate general in the capital city. At the same time, the commission informed London that the ships identified as rum-running suspects, although registered in Newfoundland, were all owned by residents of other countries.

In addition, the new Commission of Government beefed up its Customs Enforcement division, which went from one enforcement officer in St. John's to eleven. It put two customs vessels on the job and instituted a training program for its officers. The improvements resulted in a drastic reduction in rum-running out of St. John's.

Chapter 2

Al Capone's Interest in St. John's

The American Underworld in Newfoundland

Prohibition in the United States created new opportunities for organized crime to make profits even they couldn't imagine. It did not take long for the mobsters to push out the independent bootleggers and take control of the whole operation inside the United States. Their tentacles then reached into St. Pierre and Newfoundland, both of which had become legalized transhipment ports for liquor. Once it became clear that St. John's was legally an open port for the movement of liquor, they welcomed it as another St. Pierre.

During the era of Prohibition in the United States, Al Capone emerged as the top mobster in the country. His capers made international headlines. Capone controlled the politicians, police, bootleggers, prostitution and smuggling. He ruled a 1,000-man mob and his gross income was near $100 million annually.[1]

Andrew Sinclair, author of *Prohibition: The Era of Excess* wrote that the United States had great difficulty enforcing its Prohibition laws, which contributed to the rapid growth of crime. He wrote:

> Judges and prisons and policemen were few: stills and home brewers and bootleggers were many. The United States had the strongest laws and the weakest government of any highly civilized people. It also had the strongest criminal class and the weakest

1 Coffey, Thomas M. *The Long Thirst*. George McLeod Limited, Toronto. 1975.

public sentiment against them of any highly civilized people.[2]

With such a vast opportunity to easily amass great profits, ruthless gangsters began emerging throughout the country. The mobster syndicates availing of rum-running along the Atlantic coast were made up of America's most notorious gangsters of the Prohibition era. These syndicates ran the operations along Rum Row where smugglers from, or working through, St. Pierre and Newfoundland smuggled contraband liquor into the United States. They were not people to mess with and took an active interest in the operations out of both places.

The different syndicates met in Atlantic City in 1929 and formed "The Condottieri" which, among other things, acted as referees for inter-mob disputes. The move was prompted by the high rate of murders being committed by mobsters. In Capone's area alone there were 300 to 400 murders annually. The mobs were doing a $2 billion a year bootlegging business that was being threatened by the violence, as the public was turning against them. Capone was doing a short stint in prison in Philadelphia at that time. The organization included:

• Al Capone, the biggest mobster of the time who ran the Chicago operations. Likely represented by one of the Torrio brothers.
• Frank Castiglia (better known as Frank Costello), Francesco Ioele (better known as Frank Yale), Larry Fay, Owney Madden (nicknamed "The Killer") and Dutch Shultz who ran the New York mob.
• Max Hoff and the Purple Gang ran Philadelphia and area.
• The Old Remus mob ran Cincinnati and St. Louis.
• Solly Weismann was the top man for Kansas City.

2 Sinclair, Andrew. *Prohibition: The Era of Excess*. Little, Brown & Company. Boston & New York. 1962. pp371.

These mobsters looked to St. Pierre, Newfoundland and Canada to provide the rum-running operations needed to smuggle contraband liquor past the American Coast Guard while enroute to Rum Row for transfer to mob-controlled boats, which delivered it to rum-runners on American soil.

With the coming of the so-called Rum-runners Navy[3], American gangsters were able to visit the ports that warehoused their liquor before heading for Rum Row. Capone and associates chartered Newfoundland-registered vessels just for that purpose –"taking care of business."

Capone is known to have visited St. John's during his reign as mob boss, but until now the reason for the visit was merely speculation. People thought that it was a pleasure trip associated with his visit to St. Pierre to inspect the warehouses which stored his liquor. While in St. John's, he stayed at the Newfoundland Hotel and autographed a menu there which ended up in the files of the Newfoundland Historic Society.

Actually, he and the Torrio brothers chartered one of the vessels that had changed its port of registry to Newfoundland. The vessel had several Newfoundland crewmen including, Tom Power of St. John's, Newfoundland. His daughter, Kay Coady, of Kilbride revealed an interesting anecdote involving her father while he was travelling with Capone.

Tom Power, a St. John's man and Capone

Power was only eighteen years old at the time. Before Capone boarded the vessel, the captain instructed Power to wait on the mob boss and his three associates, but never to enter his quarters unless invited to do so. Kay recalled her father telling the story:

3 Eighty-one or more rum-running vessels that changed their port registrations to a Newfoundland port to make the smuggling operations run more smoothly.

They kept to themselves most of the time and didn't talk much when they came out. I was told not to speak to Capone unless he spoke to me first. There were always one or two men who stood outside his cabin guarding it. I was told to deliver the meal trays to the cabin and then leave. Occasionally, Capone would strike up a conversation and sometimes, he and his bodyguards would come up on deck and chat with the crew.

On one occasion, while the schooner was docked at St. John's, Capone, his bodyguards and two or three of the crew, including Tom Power, went ashore and ended up at a photo-shop. After Capone sat for a photo, the others followed. That is, all except for Power. When Capone asked him why he wasn't having a photo taken, he replied that he didn't have a suit. The gangster was amused by the reply and gave him an invitation he couldn't refuse. Capone invited him into the dressing room, where he removed his suit and told Power to put it on and have his picture taken. Power did. Years later, when one of his grandchildren pointed to the picture on display in

Seated is Tom Power, of St. John's who was a crewman on Capone's boat which was chartered for use by the mob for two year periods. The second photograph shows Al Capone in hat chatting with an unidentified man. Courtesy of Kay (Power) Coady.

the Power family house on Haggerty Street and asked, "Pop, how come you got a suit on there? You never wear suits." Power replied, "You wouldn't believe it if I told you."[4]

Tom Power was employed on the ship chartered by Capone from a Newfoundland-registered owner who chartered vessels to the mob during Prohibition. Information gathered suggests that Capone and associates used these vessels to travel to St. Pierre, St. John's and Port aux Basques to inspect the rum-running operations supplying Rum Row and check out their warehouses.

Legs Diamond Comes to Town

The Newfoundland Hotel was located on Cavandish Square overlooking the Furness Withy Wharf where the liquor being shipped to American gangsters was regularly unloaded and then stored in bonded warehouses in St. John's. The Torrio brothers, at the time, were acting as Capone's bodyguards. They later ventured out on their own in Brooklyn, New York, where they had associations with criminals like Dutch Shultz and Jack "Legs" Diamond.

Diamond also visited Newfoundland, but not in the company of Al Capone. Diamond was sent to Germany by Shultz to purchase $200,000 in "dope." Dope in that era had a different meaning altogether than in these modern times. Dope referred to over the counter products containing alcohol. The mobsters increased the amount of liquor in these products and easily bootlegged their products across the United States.

However, Diamond was refused entry into Germany and spent some of Shultz's money while enjoying a holiday in Europe. On his way back to New York, he hid out for a while in St. John's.

---

4 This anecdote and picture appeared in *Newfoundland Adventures*, which mistakenly identified Tom Power as Tom Coady. Coady was Kay Power's father-in-law. It was Power who travelled with Capone.

James Martin, vice president of the Longshoremen's Union in the 1950s, recalled Diamond's stay in town. "He stayed at the old Crosbie Hotel and used a taxi to get around town. He had some kind of lottery going on among the longshoremen, who numbered several thousand at the time." Martin said that Diamond was friendly and got along easily with workers on the waterfront. He was known as a good tipper. In view of his association with Dutch Shultz, he likely used the lottery profits to replenish the amount he had taken. He returned to the United States but was later gunned down at his boarding house room by two hoods. He was known as "Legs" because he was known to double-cross his friends and was always on the run.

Capone visited Halifax to meet with members of the Halifax syndicate, which played a major role in rum-running to and from Canada, St. Pierre and Newfoundland. Some of Montreal's syndicates involved with distillery plants also had agents in Halifax.

Capone and the Bank at St. Pierre

Henri Moraze, who became St. Pierre's kingpin during the era of the long thirst in most of North America, at the age of sixteen, began his career in rum-running. He started by working on vessels operating between Demerara and St. Pierre and grew with the business until he became an agent and warehouseman for Canadian interests who were cashing in on the liquor drought known as Prohibition that struck the United States. The St. Pierre government saw this as good business for the little French colony.[5]

Henri Moraze never forgot the first time he met Capone, when the famous mobster and friends arrived in St. Pierre. Around this same time, Capone had visited Halifax, Port aux Basques and other points with strong connections to the rum-

5 Calver, John. "Rumrunning in the Good Old Days" *Newfoundland Lifestyle*, 1986, Vol. 4(1), pp. 38-39.

running trade, even though Newfoundland's real connection was as well-known as that of St. Pierre.

Moraze told historian Jean P. Andrieux, "Capone was a man to be worried about. A nice fellow when you meet him, straight in business, but very, very dangerous with the gun." While in St. Pierre, Capone showed interest in a local building with bars on the window, perhaps he thought it was the local jail. After he was told it was the local bank, he seemed even more interested. Capone commented to his bodyguards, "Well, get in there and clean her out." A merchant showing him the town, nervously said, "Don't do that! I have all my money in there."[6]

The police were made aware of this by a businessman present during the conversation. Not wanting to tip their hand to Capone, the police waited until dark, then set up a team to stay inside the bank and guard it until morning. It turned out that Capone was more interested in the warehouses that stored his liquor and the operation of moving his contraband safely to Rum Row. St. Pierre need not have had any fear about Capone robbing its bank.[7]

Capone and the Cigar

Another Capone caper preserved by Andrieux was the story of Capone and the cigar. The toughest of St. Pierre's rum-running captains was introduced to Capone and the Torrio brothers, also well-known American gangsters. The captain was a non-smoker and when Capone offered him a cigar, he refused. One of the Torrio brothers stepped forward, pulled a gun and pointed at the captain's forehead. Moraze later recalled, "He eventually smoked it all with a gun to his head and a gradually paling face."[8]

6 Andrieux, Jean P. *Prohibition and St. Pierre.* pp83
7 Ibid

The most famous anecdote regarding Capone preserved by Andrieux is how Al Capone's hat became a historic artifact on St. Pierre. Andrieux stated:

> The Chicago mobsters took in shops, the distillers' offices and all the business establishments, most of which were connected with the liquor trade in one form or another. At one of the larger stores on the waterfront the employees scurried in fear, to call the manager. What does one say to a gangster without fear that a chance remark might be taken the wrong way, the storekeeper found the answer, complimenting Capone of the straw hat he was wearing. The kingpin of the underworld was pleased. 'Have it—a souvenir from Al Capone,' he quipped as he handed the man his hat.[9]

Capone's hat continues to be on display at Hotel Robert on St. Pierre as an artifact from the days of rum-running and gangsters, when St. Pierre was one of the most important links in the chain of supplying rum to bootleggers in the United States.

St. John's Man at Capone Shootout

Ben Strickland of St. John's was well-known around town in the 1930s. He was a popular fellow at parties because of his charming talent of being able to uplift the mood by telling jokes, leading a sing-song or adding a musical accompaniment to anyone playing an instrument. In those days, the instrument was usually: a mouth organ, accordion, piano or banjo. Ben played none of these instruments, but had a reputation as "the best spoons player" in town. He found these skills an

8 Ibid
9 Ibid

asset when, during the Great Depression days, he ended up in Chicago. While frequenting one of the famous speakeasies there during Prohibition, he encountered, and became friends with, members of the Capone mob. It did not take long for this young Newfoundlander to find himself an active member of the mob.

When interviewed in the late 1960s in St. John's, he recalled those days in Chicago.

> There was this party one night where the room was filled with smoke, lots of liquor, and many guests with friends in the mob. When the piano player started up, things quietened down and I pulled the spoons out of my pocket and played along with him. It was a catchy tune and when it ended, everyone clapped. They really enjoyed it. Then a lady guest there, Sophie Tucker, a very famous entertainer, who was invited out of the audience to sing. She asked if I would play the spoons along with the piano player and I said, 'Not a problem, Ma'am.' It was great bit of fun.[10]

Strickland remembered, "Sometimes it got scary." He told of being in a car with other armed mob members when they were ordered to follow behind Capone's car on some business Capone was carrying out. He said that Capone had bodyguards in his car with him. Strickland stated, "On the way back he pulled into a drugstore. Just as he was near the door to go in, a car pulled around a corner and fired at him as it passed. Luckily no one was hurt."

Ben Strickland was later picked up by police after a man was found in a field not far from the drugstore having been stabbed with a pitchfork. "I had nothing to do with that and

---

10 Sophie Tucker later made a movie with Frank Sinatra, and appeared on top television shows including "The Ed Sullivan Show."

was not charged, but they were sure Capone's gang was behind it. I was deported because of it though," concluded Strickland.

Was Capone Insane or a Criminal Genius?

Author and researcher Marc Mappen examined the long-standing question which asked, "Setting syphilis aside, was Al Capone a criminal genius or just a lug who had gotten lucky?"

Some of the opinions he collected came down on both sides of the debate:

• Thomas Reppetto in his book, *American Mafia*, referred to Capone as a thug who lacked business skills.

• Jay Robert Nash said, "Capone was a murderous thug without remorse, a near illiterate who acquired countless millions and knew not where to spend a dime of it. Worse, for a decade the city of Chicago embraced this bragging boasting, struttin' killer."

• Stephen Fox said, "He was a stupid chuckleheaded buffoon, thrashing flailing white elephant whom even his friends gave a wide berth."

Arguments from the opposing view:

• Arthur Madden, a federal treasury agent who investigated Capone said, "Capone was a fathead."

• New York mobster Joe Bonnano observed, "In Italian Capone's name translated to 'castrated male chicken.'"

• His first biographer, Fred Palau, said, "He was Neapolitan by birth and Neanderthal by instinct."

Another side:

Biographer Robert Schoenberg argued he was more imaginative and intelligent than most criminals of that era. He tried to portray himself as a loving family man and civic-minded benefactor who wanted to achieve lasting peace between warring mobs. Capone said that public service was his motto.

Schoenberg gave a couple of examples to demonstrate Al Capone's agility of mind:

In court, Capone was on trial for being caught with a concealed weapon. After finding him guilty and levying a fine, the judge commented, "Maybe this will be a lesson to you."

"Yes, judge, it certainly will. I'll never tote a gun again... in Joliet."

In another anecdote, he noted that when Capone started his career in Chicago he ran a whorehouse called the Four Deuces Brothel. When asked his profession, he answered:

"I'm a dealer in second hand furniture." Capone answered.

"What kind of stuff do you sell?"

"Any old thing a man might want to lie on."[11]

Capone Defended his Reputation

In his later years, Capone showed contempt for big business and particularly big newspapers. He told a reporter:

I didn't interfere with big business. None of the big business guys can say I ever took a dollar from 'em. I done a favour for one of the big newspapers in the country when they was up against it. Broke a strike for 'em, and what do I get for doing 'em a favour? Here they've been ever since, clamped on my back. I only want to do business, you understand, with my own class. Why can't they leave me alone? I don't interfere with them any. Get me? I don't interfere with their racket. They should let my racket be.[12]

11 Mappen, Marc. *Prohibition Gangsters: The Rise and Fall of a Bad Generation* . Rutgers University Press, New Brunswick, New Jersey and London, 2013.
12 Sinclair, Andrew. *Prohibition: The Era of Excess*. Little, Brown & Co. 1962.

Capone insisted that he always dealt fairly with, "… the poor and drunkers."

Rum-runners of St. John's

Although St. Pierre was free from Prohibition, which made it the rum-runners "Jewel" of the Atlantic, it had one drawback which tended to push St. John's up the scale of choice sites for criminals to deal with.

St. John's already had established a profitable trade with the British colony of Guyana for Demerara rum. The drinking public in Newfoundland and the east coast of the United States and Canada favoured Demerara rum. Unfortunately for St. Pierre, French law did not allow the import of rum from Demerara, because they wanted to protect the sales of rum from the French Caribbean.

Historian Jean P. Andrieux noted,

> This gave rise to St. John's, Newfoundland, as the centre for warehousing of the most notable product of Britain's South American colony. Warehouses of Eastern Trading Co and Tessier & Co. held large stocks of Demerara rum. Schooners loaded at St. John's and cleared for the high seas. Once outside the three-mile limit there were ingenious methods used to return the rum to eager buyers in the island Dominion or on Canadian shores.[13]

Gangsters Chartered Newfoundland Schooners

During Prohibition in the United States there were plenty of sailing ships, mostly schooners, in Newfoundland that were involved in the fish export business. Some owners earned

13 Andrieux, Jean Pierre. *Prohibition and St. Pierre.*

extra money by chartering their vessels to members of the American, Halifax and Montreal syndicates for rum-running. The Moultons' of Burgeo had four stern schooners involved in rum-running. Vessels leaving Newfoundland ports or Nova Scotia, would list their destinations as Nassau or Havana but the actual destination would be Rum Row, in waters just outside territorial limits where American gangsters would be waiting to unload them.

The *Edna A. Moulton* was a Newfoundland-registered vessel with a Newfoundland crew. It had been built in Isaacs Cove, Nova Scotia, in 1919 for J.T. Moulton Company of Burgeo and was 204 tons. It was used as a fishing schooner until 1923, when it was chartered to a rum-running syndicate to be used during Prohibition. In one trip, the *Edna* smuggled 7,000 cases as well as 200 kegs of liquor. Although it carried a clearance certificate for Havana, it was delivered to awaiting smugglers at Rum Row. During the tough economic times of Prohibition, some Newfoundlanders turned to the rum-running trade to make a living. Several Newfoundlanders claimed to have worked with the Al Capone organization in Chicago, and were deported from the United States for their involvement.[14]

Captain John "Machine Gun" Kelly

A colourful anecdote of the Prohibition era involved Captain John Kelly, who was one of several men who held the position of captain on the *Nellie J. Banks*. The conspiracy trials being conducted in Canada were making all those involved in rum-running nervous and, as told elsewhere in this book, got the attention of mobsters in the United States.

During testimony in court a witness implicated the *Nellie J. Banks*, when Captain John Kelly, alias John "Machine Gun" Kelly, took the stand. A brief reference in records, noted that

14 Thorne, Robert. "The Rumrunners of Burgeo." *Downhomer*, January 1999, Vol. 11(8), pp. 118-119.

Kelly got the name "Machine Gun" Kelly after firing a machine gun off in Lunenburg, Nova Scotia, which killed a man. It appears to have been written off as an accidental shooting as records indicate he continued to work as a captain on rum-runners without any mention of an arrest, imprisonment or trial.

Whether he was the same "Machine Gun" Kelly involved with the American mobs and made famous in Hollywood movies about mobsters and Prohibition was not mentioned, nor confirmed.

Kelly described seeing the *Nellie J. Banks* during a storm when he was taking his own schooner to shore to wait out the bad weather. One way of identifying a rum-runner beyond the territorial limits at that time was that during inclement weather the rum-runner was forced to stay put because going to the nearest port with a cargo of rum ran a high risk of being arrested.[15]

Gunfire at Corner Brook

Prohibition was a difficult period for the constabulary due to a lack of resources. Enforcement of the new law was near impossible in outports where one man, a political appointment, would serve as justice of the peace, customs officer, and oftentimes held the duties of telegraph officer. As mentioned earlier, in the capital city, St. John's could boast of only one inspector of customs, one inspector of preventative service, a clerk and surveyor of shipping, one registrar of shipping and one customs officer. This must have really intimidated the gangster bootleggers like Al Capone, Dutch Shultz, Legs Diamond, and even Rocco Perri in Toronto, Canada's answer to Capone.

The Newfoundland government was better organized to collect customs duties, as opposed to rooting out the rum-

15 Calver, John. "Rumrunning in the Good Old Days." *Newfoundland Lifestyle*, 1986, Vol. 4(1), pp. 38-39.

runners. In 1926-1927 there were customs collectors in 145 outport communities. On the west coast, the customs inspector, after learning that the rum-running vessel the *Marion and Rita* was off the coast, near Corner Brook had no boat to use to make an arrest. He had to hire a private tugboat to take him out. As the little boat moved in on the rum-runners, they were forced to take cover from the spray of bullets fired from the schooner. A chase followed but the little tug was outclassed by the rum-runners who got away. The captain later explained that he thought the tug was carrying modern day pirates who wanted to steal their ship.[16]

The Cluetts

Two fishing captains living in St. John's, Bill and Alf Cluett, were among the large number of Newfoundlanders attracted to the rum-running trade during the Capone Prohibition era. They operated independently from any criminal syndicate and faced danger not only of being caught by the Coast Guard but also from the many vessels that operated along Rum Row and were owned by American gangsters.

Despite the high risks, the Cluetts managed to dodge interference from the Coast Guard and Capone's hoods for more than five years. However, their good luck changed on the morning of January 25, 1931. That was the day an American Coast Guard cutter pulled alongside their *Josephine K.*, and without any warning fired shots across her bow. The first shot missed hitting the vessel, however, the second went through the wheelhouse window and into the chest of Captain Bill Cluett.

Cluett dropped to the floor immediately and his ship was brought to a stop. In rapid succession, members of the Coast Guard stormed aboard the vessel with guns drawn and ready to fire. The twenty-five-man Cluett crew, which included four

16 Hunter, Mark. *Prohibition.* p 46.

Newfoundlanders, were all placed under arrest and taken to New York where they were imprisoned. Captain Cluett was rushed to a nearby hospital but died shortly after being admitted.

Meanwhile, Alf Cluett was released on bail and joined other family members from Newfoundland, who were going to Lunenburg, Nova Scotia, where Bill's wife and family lived, to be with them for Bill's funeral services.

The incident captured international headlines and within hours of Cluett's death, the British and Canadian governments expressed grave concern over the killing and claimed it occurred outside the twelve-mile limit. The American government responded by ordering an immediate enquiry into the incident.

"Bill Cluett was a good husband, a good father, a good friend and a master mariner," family friend Reverend E. Ryder stated in his eulogy at the funeral services.

"Bill Cluetts death was nothing less than murder on the high seas. This was one of the inevitable tragedies that follow the hypocrisy of Prohibition," Ryder concluded.

Upon returning to St. John's, the Cluetts spoke openly about their involvement in rum-running. Mrs. Cluett said she was proud of her surviving son, Alf, but wanted him to retire from the illegal trade. Alf disregarded her advice. He returned to being a rum-runner because he loved the excitement associated with it.

The American enquiry into the incident exonerated the Coast Guard and found that Bill Cluett's death was the result of an accidental shooting that occurred while the Coast Guard was affecting a legal arrest.

Early in the winter of 1929, an incident occurred in a St. Pierre bar that one could only imagine happening in Chicago, perhaps because it involved two American rum-runners working for the syndicates.

Nick Makris, alias Nick Carros, a crewman on a vessel in port unloading a cargo of liquor designed for Rum Row, left his ship that night with one object in mind — to find Gustav Karlsen. Karlsen was a ships' engineer who had arrived in port earlier that day. For some reason, never explained, bad blood existed between the two, and Makris was determined to settle the score in a permanent manner.

Nick traced Karlsen to a crowded, smoke-filled bar. He stopped momentarily while his eyes scanned the room intently until resting on his victim standing at the bar. His hand went into his pocket as he made his way towards Karlsen. Without any prior conversation or warning, Nick quickly pointed his gun at Karlsen and pulled the trigger. The bullet penetrated the victim's chest causing him to fall to the floor. The crackling sound of gunfire brought momentary silence inside the bar. Nick wasted no time. While attempting to leave, Knute Henderson, a friend of the victim, tried to stop him but a second shot was fired by Makris which wounded Henderson, who fell helpless to the floor. Karlsen died later in hospital.

Makris made a successful escape from the bar and evaded a massive police hunt, which covered the entire island and lasted several days. During the search, none of the ships in port were permitted to leave. However, due to the pressure on business caused by the port being closed down, the ban was lifted.

Although St. Pierre is a tiny island, Nick Makris was never found. Yet, Makris was tried in absentia on March 18, 1929. The hood was found guilty of murder and sentenced to life imprisonment. By this time, the guillotine had been abandoned by St. Pierre justice. Makris, some believe, had entered the United States through Rum Row, where he continued his association with the mob. He had successfully evaded police with the help of shipmates, who hid him in a rolled up sail during the police hunt.

"The Noxious Concoctions of the U.S. Underworld"

The mobsters controlling the illegal liquor trade during Prohibition sometimes had to turn to manufacturing their own homemade brews for distribution when the contraband shipments from Newfoundland, St. Pierre and Canada were interrupted or delayed. This proved to be risky business because of the high risk of injury or death caused by the consumption of these products. However, there were enormous profits being made by supplying booze to the U.S., which is why the mob, when necessary, turned to making moonshine, swamp whisky, bathtub gin and needled beer, a product made by adding raw alcohol to the near beer allowed by American law.

These amateur moonshiners showed little concern for the fact that adding wood alcohol to ethyl alcohol made it toxic and unfit for human consumption. They would try to remove any risks by putting the product through a second refining process. This process was an improvement, but there remained a high risk that consumption could cause blindness and even death.

C.W Hunter, the author of *Booze, Boats and Billions*, explained:

> Problems sometimes arose when the raw alcohol had not been properly denatured and contained quantities of wood alcohol. Organized crime had little or no concern for sanitation—dead rats were found in every one of a hundred barrels of mash confiscated by one Chicago policeman. Death from alcohol poisonings in the USA shot up from 1,064 in 1920 to 4,154 in 1925. Little wonder Canadian whisky, no matter how raw, commanded premium prices.

Hunter pointed out that the rum-runners supplying professionally manufactured alcohol beverages, "...provided

American drinkers with a safe alternative to the noxious concoctions of the U.S. underworld." During the Prohibition years in Newfoundland, some imbibers[17] turned to using wood alcohol and died as a result.

17 Drinkers

Chapter 3

Undercover Agent
Double-Crosses the Mob

In late 1935, Captain Israel Lillington of Port aux Basques, headed a rum-running effort to move illegal rum stored in St. Pierre to Sydney, Nova Scotia. He had expert help from the Halifax syndicate, who efficiently organized a small fleet of speed boats which were utilized to swiftly transport the cargo from a point outside the three-mile limit to destinations on shore.[1] The operation was successful mainly because it caught the R.C.M.P. offguard. It was an unexpected move.

During Prohibition, rum-running was a major concern of authorities in the United States and Canada. In those desperate times, many Newfoundland fishermen turned to rum-running to supplement their meagre income. To combat the hugely profitable rum-running activity, Canadian and American authorities combined their efforts in an intelligence operation to intercept these illegal operations.

One of the Canadian restrictions required that vessels obtain custom's clearance to permit fishermen of Newfoundland and Nova Scotia to unload their catches, providing that the vessel did not call at any foreign port before returning to home port.

The captain of the *Nellie J. Banks* was Israel Lillington. Although Lillington was part of the two-nation anti-rum smuggling operation, officials did not trust him. They had good reason because, unknown to them at the time, he was playing a double role and using the cover given him to bootleg rum. Canadian customs learned about Lillington's double role

---

1 Although the three-mile limit still applied in Canadian and Newfoundland waters, the United States, with approval of Britain, extended the limit to twelve miles to better battle Prohibition.

through, "...a loose lips sinks ship" sort of incident. At the time, the *Nellie J. Banks* was operating as a decoy just outside the three-mile limit.

While in port at Port aux Basques, one of his crewmen was overheard bragging in a tavern that they had just come from St. Pierre, which was a major drop off and storage point for rum being smuggled into Canada and the United States. The tip went through official intelligence sources all the way to Washington and Ottawa. Agents policing the Canadian and Newfoundland coasts were alerted and gave special attention to their prized decoy.

Rum-runners Organized

Just as the authorities were well-organized, so were the rum-runners. The Halifax syndicate had developed a strategic plan to circumvent the Coast Guard and successfully deliver the rum supplies, some of which were destined for Chicago, to Boston, New York, Nova Scotia and Prince Edward Island. The syndicate employed mobile radio operators using special codes and placed under the control of knowledgeable experts who guided these schooners carrying contraband cargoes to their destinations.

When the Coast Guard surprised a rum-runner, a standard tactic of the targeted crew was to toss kegs of liquor overboard with the intentions of fouling up the cutters long enough to escape.

The syndicate bosses had the aid of lawyers whose expertise included knowing the loopholes in the law. A major commandment issued to all captains supplying the syndicate was, "Do not get caught inside territorial limits," which were three miles off the coast at that time.

Some of the Newfoundland captains involved with the syndicate often played cat and mouse with the Coast Guard. Frequently, the schooner would occupy a specific spot outside the three-mile limit and use the vessel as a floating tavern. Their customers were pre-advised of the ship's arrival and were left to find their own way to visit and avail of its service. Outside the limits, they could drink as much as they wanted. The purchase price for a gallon of rum in the 1930s was four dollars and a quart of brandy went for one dollar.

Captain Lillington's involvement in being a decoy for authorities, in waters just outside the limits, gave him the advantage of knowing just where the cutters were hanging out. Whenever he was ready to operate his floating bar, he would radio the Coast Guard a false report of "All clear. No sign of rum-runners." While the cutters were receiving these messages, small motor boats were arriving from land with customers, including businessmen and politicians, to enjoy some genuine Demerara rum.

In 1936, on the night of the world championship boxing match between Joe Louis and Schmeling, the Coast Guard cutters were miles away from the *Nellie J. Banks*, thanks to the reports received from their decoy.

Meanwhile, Captain Lillington, after declaring "Bar Open!" turned the ships radio on full blast for the enjoyment of his guests. The much anticipated championship fight was a big draw that night. Such was the era of Prohibition. The bar remained open until Schmeling knocked out the great Joe Louis in the twelfth round. It was a profitable night for the rum-runners, and what was left over was easily marketed in St. Pierre. From there, the captain returned to Port aux Basques.

Lillington, still confident he had outsmarted the authorities, had not banked on an astute official in Port aux Basques who, after searching the schooner for contraband and finding none, was about to leave a smiling Lillington behind when he stopped, turned to the captain and commented, "I see you had good fishing captain."

"In that we did, young fella," replied the captain, still not suspecting anything was amiss.

The official left Lillington wide-eyed and open-mouthed when he firmly stated, "Well, in that case, I am going to place you under arrest and seize your ship."

Under Canadian law, Newfoundland vessels could fish in Canadian waters but were not permitted to stop at any foreign port before delivering their catch.

He went on to explain why he was making the arrest. "Contrary to your claim, this vessel, sir, was not involved in any fishing. See there, the dories are all dry, the hooks and lines were never used."

Things continued to unravel for the captain of the *Nellie J. Banks*. The official searched the captain's quarters and found that the efficient rum-runner had maintained a written record of his customers, including a list of the rum he had returned to St. Pierre.

Lillington's temper flared and his finest efforts to intimidate the inspector completely failed. Customs officials, in accordance with arrest procedures, removed the mainsail and part of the ship's engine, which assured the vessel would not be moved from its moorings.

Lillington was a realist and when shouting, threats and verbal intimidation failed, he followed the last rule to apply in such a set of circumstances.

"I'm packing my bags and going to St. John's to hire the best lawyer I can find," he told his crew. He already had a lawyer in mind. John McEvoy had a fine reputation among sea captains as a man who knew well the customs laws of Canada.

A telegraph from McEvoy to customs in Port aux Basques, and to the federal prosecutor, resulted in the immediate release of the vessel. However, an important condition was attached. Customs intended to charge the captain with having made a false declaration, when he denied he had not been to St. Pierre to drop of his rum cargo. McEvoy had convinced them to release the vessel and said he would deal with the charges at a later date. In return, his client would plead guilty.

In November, 1936, the case was heard and over lunch McEvoy and the prosecutor worked out a satisfactory deal acceptable to both sides. McEvoy had stressed that customs had no evidence that Lillington had stopped at St. Pierre other than the word of the inspector, who was not on St. Pierre and was relying on hearsay. Lillington pleaded guilty and gladly paid half of the usual fine for the offence.

With his legal problem out of the way, Lillington rushed back to Port aux Basques and secured the release of his vessel. He wasted little time getting back into the rum-running operation.

As authorities concentrated their efforts on St. Pierre, the smuggling of rum became more difficult. Fewer Newfoundland captains became involved in the illegal operations. The *Nellie J. Banks* was not one of them. Lillington had learned his lesson. He told his men, "I won't be caught offguard like that again." Once his schooner was ready to sail, he headed straight out to sea. At this time, the larger vessels had just about replaced the three-mast schooners in trafficking rum from Demerara.

Lillington survived by smuggling illegal liquor to a string of bootleggers on Prince Edward Island. He renewed his floating tavern operation and spread the word around the Island. He provided live accordion music for the entertainment of his patrons. The successful combination of toe-tapping music and flowing liquor created a party atmosphere in which the locals added step dancing to their rum guzzling. Among his first guests was a senator from Prince Edward Island.

Organized Crime Moves In

By this time, there were two organizations controlling the rum-running business. In addition to the Halifax syndicate, there was a Cape Breton mob.[2] Lillington was adept in avoiding confrontations with both of them. However, he

2 Robinson, George and Dorothy. *The Nellie J. Banks.* Self-published. 1970. p79

was always prepared in case thugs were sent out to disrupt his operations. He always had a loaded rifle nearby, and was heard to comment, "The first one to come after me will find himself a stranger in heaven." This was the same threat he sometimes made to customs officials attempting to take his ship when he felt they had no cause.

Lillington was known for his floating tavern, particularly on nights when a professional boxing match was being broadcasted. It was a spirited night on the *Nellie J. Banks* during the broadcast of the fight between Joe Louis and Jack Farr.

A soused Lillington got carried away by the broadcasters exciting description of the fight and tossed a powerful punch, inadvertently stepped into by the ship's cook, John Clothier of Port aux Basques. His fist caught Clothier on the forehead and knocked him out a cold junk. A fellow crewman quipped, "No flipper dinner tonight." The cook was famous for his specialty, seal flipper dinners.

The spring of 1938 marked the beginning of the end for the most famous little rum-running ship in the business, the *Nellie J. Banks*. The schooner departed from Port aux Basques with the brandy-drinking, hot-tempered Captain Lillington in command, and his Newfoundland crew of John Clothier, Alfred Matthews and James Bird.

Their first stop was St. Pierre, where the contact for rum-runners was Henri Moraze. Henri operated a mother ship, a three-masted schooner called the *Greta Kure*, which he used to bring alcohol from Denmark to St. Pierre, destined for bootleggers, speakeasies and nightclubs in the United States and Canada.

While Captain Lillington knew his way around the rum-running business, and had a rough and ready ability of dealing with unruly people including custom officers, he was illiterate. Although the Canadian government had recently passed a law extending the three-mile territorial limit to twelve miles,

Lillington had no knowledge of the change. It was business as usual for him.

The new law was the result of a negotiated agreement between Great Britain and Canada which permitted Canadian officials to board, search and arrest vessels hovering within twelve miles of the Canadian coastline.

Chapter 4

Canadian Crime Syndicates Go International

There were crime syndicates operating in Halifax, Cape Breton and Montreal with connections in Port aux Basques and St. John's, Newfoundland. In addition to their involvement in delivering contraband to the American market, the syndicates were also playing a part in supplying booze to the Canadian provinces, which were under Prohibition, as well as enabling legitimate distillers in Canada to circumvent excise taxes.

These operations were threatened when eight men in Montreal, including distillery owners the Bronfman brothers, were arrested on conspiracy charges. The investigation revealed that the Montreal group had agents in Halifax. The police believed that these contacts were working with the Montreal syndicate by accepting, legally, shipments of liquor from Montreal and using the vessels of the other accused to return that same cargo to Canada as part of a scheme to avoid paying excise taxes. This developing police investigation caused uneasiness among the American mobs, which worried about how the outcome would affect the delivery of liquor to the United States. Smuggling rum into the United States during Prohibition involved a widespread international organization, often using elaborate and sophisticated methods to assure successful delivery of liquor supplies to an enormously profitable market. Key to mob interests were the islands of St. Pierre and Newfoundland. The American mobs took more than a passing interest when made aware that police were digging into records in both places.

R.C.M.P. Investigates

The R.C.M.P. took over the enforcement of Canada's customs and excise laws in 1932, and were shocked when they uncovered the extent and organization of rum-running involving Nova Scotia, Prince Edward Island, Newfoundland, not yet a Canadian province, and St. Pierre. Rum-running historian Geoff Robinson explained:

> It was a gigantic conspiracy to evade excise law. Having been exported duty free from Canada to St. Pierre, large amounts of liquor were returned to Canada via several groups of Maritimers [Newfoundland included] and others who owned vessels. Thus, in the numbers and diversity of persons involved, this case stands out as one of the most unusual in Canadian Criminal Law.

Among those targeted were four brothers in the famous Bronfman family of Montreal and three others in Montreal all linked with, "…a man in Perth, Scotland, a man in Newfoundland, one in British Columbia and two men in St. Pierre."[1] The Bronfmans often sought the counsel of a businessman in St. John's. The man referred to was likely a businessman with powerful political influence and an interest in the production, marketing and distribution of alcoholic beverages, and who also possessed a superior knowledge of Newfoundland's customs and excise laws.

1 Robinson, Geoff and Dorothy. *The Nellie J. Banks: Rum-Running to Prince Edward Island.* Self-published. 1970.

Off Come the Gloves

Some captains in the fleet of rum-runners followed a pattern of behaviour aimed at slowing down and obstructing police. When such confrontations took place, the captain followed an aggressive course of action aimed at resolving the matter. First, he would try to be intimidating by verbally abusing authorities attempting to board his ship.

If that failed, he turned up the obstruction antics by becoming more threatening. Sometimes it worked, usually when the officials had not been able to produce a search warrant. Most often it only gained the crew a little time to get rid of records. When the stalling tactics proved to be a complete failure, only one course of action remained. As Newfoundland Captain Israel Lillington, who had the system down pat, often said, "Retreat, pack your bags and rush to St. John's to see a lawyer." For him that was John McEvoy.

While Captain Lillington knew his way around the rum-running business and had a rough and ready ability of dealing with crewmen and custom officers, he was illiterate. Although the Canadian government had recently passed an act extending the three-mile territorial limit to twelve miles and had this new law gazetted, thereby making it the law, Lillington was totally in the dark on the matter and it was business as usual for him. The new law was the result of a negotiated agreement between Great Britain and Canada, which permitted Canadian officials to board, search and arrest vessels hovering within twelve miles of the Canadian coastline.

Makes History

The *Nellie J. Banks* became the first vessel to be charged with violating the new twelve-mile limit law. A surveillance plane spotted the rum-runner and alerted the R.C.M.P. cutter *Ulna,* which charted a direct course to intercept its target.

When the R.C.M.P. arrived and boarded the schooner, Captain Lillington had to be awakened by his crew. He was startled to see the police already on board and showed his annoyance by growling, "Yes, I have a cargo of liquor, rum and tobacco from St. Pierre on board but I am well outside the three-mile limit." The arresting officer was happy to point out, "You are actually eight miles outside."

He then explained the new twelve-mile limit and seized the vessel and its cargo. The schooner was then towed to Charlottetown. Lillington clammed up and refused to cooperate with the police. It was time to consult his lawyer in St. John's.

The *Banks* was seized and taken to Nova Scotia where the Newfoundland crew was deported back to Newfoundland. Bird, a crewman from Port aux Basques and a talented accordion player, managed to smuggle, right under the nose of his captors, some of the contraband cargo. He did this by stuffing tobacco inside the accordion, and bid goodbye to the police officers as he headed home.

This was a critical arrest for the R.C.M.P. because it put them on the path to uncovering a large rum-running conspiracy.

R.C.M.P. Surprised by the Size of the Conspiracy

When the R.C.M.P. first suspected that a conspiracy to avoid paying Canada's excise and customs taxes was operating, they tread lightly in their investigation. The investigators proceeded carefully so they wouldn't alert the participants in the conspiracy. They did not anticipate that bank managers might stall their search and even tip off the suspects, which is actually what happened.

Their first visit was to the bankers in St. Pierre and Newfoundland to gather any signed and cashed cheques along with documents containing signatures that could confirm their suspicions of a conspiracy, and provide proof to support arrests.

The bankers leaked the information to intermediaries with Montreal connections so that it got to the top people in the syndicate. As a result, there was sufficient time for most records to be destroyed and for incriminating evidence from safety deposit boxes and office vaults to be moved or destroyed. However, there was not enough time to destroy all the records, and police were successful in securing these. Cashed cheques and telegrams passed between the conspirators was what they needed, and that was exactly what they found.

The R.C.M.P. initiated its sweep of arrests, which led to the largest criminal case of its kind in Canadian history with sixty-two arrests being made, including the Newfoundland crew of the *Nellie J. Banks*. By the time they began rounding up the conspirators, Ray Clarke, the real owner of the *Nellie J. Banks*, as far as police could determine, had emerged as one of the big wheels in the rum-running organization.

The *Nellie J. Banks*, the smallest vessel in the entire smuggling operation, had played a key role in uncovering the conspiracy set-up. The police, after learning that its Newfoundland owner was a fox breeder named Ray Clarke, were led to other connections showing there was a large organization implicated in a conspiracy to circumvent Canadian laws.[2]

Robinson described the case as, "One of the most unusual in Canadian Criminal law because of the numbers and the people involved."[3]

The Story Breaks Internationally

The breaking story of "A Big Rum-running Conspiracy" captured headlines across Canada, Newfoundland and the United States. After all, the United States and some European

2 Newfoundland's little rum-running schooner the *Nellie J. Banks* earned a place in Prohibition history and was subjected to international attention due to the Canadian Parliamentary Committee's 1934 investigation into rum-running that led to Royal Commission being set up in 1935.
3 Ibid

countries, not to mention Newfoundland and St. Pierre, were involved in the massive rum-running operations on the North Atlantic. More than a few Newfoundlanders watched with apprehension as details of the investigation emerged in the press.

An indication of how the wealthy and influential were treated in that era was reflected in the initial "tread lightly kid glove handling" accorded some of the top people accused of being involved.

Once the decision to lay charges was made, instead of an all-out police roundup of "the sixty-two," which would have attracted country-wide media attention, a rather surprising method of bringing lawbreakers to justice was followed. The R.C.M.P. contacted each person individually and offered each the opportunity to go to Montreal and voluntarily surrender to police. The trip to Montreal and hotel stay was paid for by the police.

Those who accepted had access to liquor on the trip, and at a stop along the way one of the officers accompanying the group picked up more liquor to replenish supplies. The method of arresting those involved in the conspiracy was justified by pointing out that it would have been far more costly to follow the normal procedure of arrest. All those who responded were brought before a judge immediately and given bail to return home for Christmas, after agreeing to voluntarily return for trial in mid-January.

The arrangement was exposed when a group of ordinary fishermen in Prince Edward Island became rebellious when offered the same deal. They went public and told their story to the press. On December 21st their answer appeared as a front page headline in newspapers, "If you want us, come and get us!"[4] If the chief aim of the "tread lightly tactic" was to avoid sensational and international headlines, it had failed.

4 The Prince Edward Island *Guardian*, December 21, 1934

The lawyer for these defendants worked out a deal with police to allow the men to remain with their families for Christmas, providing that they turn up at police barracks in Charlottetown on Christmas night. Any expectations of being released to go home after showing up were dashed when police officers surrounded and arrested them.

Ray Clarke, a top man in the syndicate, was given a cell with the comforts of a bed, while the others spent an uncomfortable night sleeping in the reception room of the Queen's County Jail on Prince Edward Island. Clarke indicated that the group expected to be provided with lawyers by the Halifax syndicate.

The lawyer for the men made a plea for mercy to be shown to his clients. He argued:

> I feel the Court should know we are rather on the fringe of things down there in a very isolated position. We have a prohibition law, so that it seems that we must have some bootleggers among our local characters. My clients are sure that they have no outside contacts. Things are far from prosperous; we are only getting ten cents for our potatoes; I mention these things in order that your Honour, in his clemency, may be able to arrange for a reasonable cash bail.[5]

The judge agreed, and the men were free to go home until the trial date. Ironically, although these men were known rum-runners and Prohibition was still law, plenty of liquor was available at their hotel. One man got soused, fell asleep in the bath and flooded his room and the rooms below.

The train that took them back to Montreal in January for trial had plenty of bootleg liquor on board, which contributed to the party atmosphere of the trip. At trial, Captain Lillington of the *Nellie J. Banks*, himself a Newfoundlander, claimed to

5 Robinson, Geoff and Dorothy. *The Nellie J. Banks*. self-published.

reside on Prince Edward Island. Police looked into his claim and confirmed that he had never lived there.

The Trial Begins

The subsequent trials began in confusion, not only because of the number of accused prisoners but because many of the offences had occurred in several other countries. To simplify the process, the judge reduced the number of charges to cover only those which violated Canadian law. Conspiracy on its own is a difficult charge to prove. Legally defined, conspiracy occurs when two or more people come together to deliberately carry out an illegal act. Such offences are often difficult to prove because the perpetrators avoid putting their agreement and plans in writing.

Lawyers for the defendants were delighted when the charges were changed from smuggling to conspiracy to smuggle. The change left little doubt that the Crown would have a difficult time proving its charges because most of the paperwork had disappeared.

The conspirators were well-represented at trial by A. Geoffrion, an acknowledged expert on Canada's customs and excise laws. The fishermen in the Maritime Provinces, who did the legwork in the rum-running operation, were not called as witnesses because the judge ruled that it was out of his jurisdiction to call them. This led to the charges being dismissed.

Historian Robinson explained:

> It might be said that the Montreal group were charged with allegedly exporting liquor out of Canada, whilst the eleven charged in Halifax were allegedly returning it thereby defrauding Canada of excise duty. So-called co-conspirators were never brought to court. It would be fair to comment that a small number of the eleven

headed up the organization for bringing the Canadian liquor, together with Demerara rum into Canada, whilst the reminder traded with them to supply their areas.[6]

Captains Israel Lillington of Port aux Basque and Ray Clarke were called to testify when those from Nova Scotia, Prince Edward Island and Newfoundland were being charged. Apparently not all the paper trails in the case had been destroyed, and a few telegrams exchanged between these two and the syndicate were submitted as evidence.

Humour in Court

Due to the widespread publicity the rum-running trials had received, the courtroom in Halifax was filled to capacity on the day the trial opened. Fishermen involved in the illegal operations were less sophisticated than the men at top levels in the organization. This resulted in frequent bursts of humour throughout the trial. Robinson noted, "The court started out like that of a convention in its light-heartedness, deteriorating to out and out comedy. There were times when the court was in danger of being cleared."[7]

Such was the case when C. Abbott, who frequented the *Nellie J. Banks* when it operated an open tavern outside the three-mile limit, testified. His testimony was expected to support the accuracy of important elements of the Crown's case. Lillington had asked Abbott to send a request for rum supplies from what the conspirators called the "Mother ships," which carried rum cargoes and remained outside the three-mile limit. The man Abbott communicated with was Ray Clarke. The defence lawyer attempted to discredit the witness by testing the reliability of his memory.

6 Robinson, Geoff and Dorothy. *The Nellie J. Banks.* Self-published.
7 Ibid

"What memory do you have of attending school," the lawyer asked Abbott.

"I remember that I really enjoyed history and that was my best subject, sir!" the witness proudly replied.

The lawyer was surprised and pleased by this answer because it gave him an opportunity to attack his credibility.

"Then tell me, sir, what date did Caesar invade Britain?"

"Hmmmm, can't remember that one, sir."

"What date was the Battle of Hastings?"

"I don't know, sir."

"Do you know then, the date of the Battle of Waterloo?"

"Can't say I do," replied the witness in a less confident tone then he had started with. The repeated outbursts of laughter in the court showed that spectators were enjoying the line of questioning.

"Well, can you tell this Court then, under what flag is Canada ruled?"

"That's easy enough sir, the Union Jack!"

Some spectators clapped their hands, which drew a smile from the witness and a warning from the judge to clear the courtroom if necessary.

"One more question, sir. What date did Napoleon retreat to Moscow?"

"Now on that one sir, I have some memory of why he retreated, but can't remember the date."

"The prosecution must think we are all gullible if they want us to believe that this witness could remember what was in the telegrams."

He then passed the witness the telegrams he had sent ordering more rum for Captain Lillington and asked him to read two paragraphs from them. After completing the reading, the lawyer took back the telegraphs and asked the witness to tell the court what the two paragraphs stated. The witness gave a hesitant, mixed-up answer.

By the time the lawyer finished cross-examining Abbott, he had completely destroyed his credibility.

Threatens Custom Officials

While the trial was going on, the *Nellie J. Banks* was left under the command of Captain Ed Dicks. As per the usual practice, Dicks repeatedly refused to allow the customs officer on board to take control of the vessel.

Finally, a Mr. Barbour, and several officials representing customs, tried to board the vessel and were obstructed from doing so by the captain. Barbour firmly told Captain Dicks, "I have been instructed by Ottawa to order you and your crew off ship immediately. And I'll use force if necessary!"

Dicks and his men were in the process of gathering things to remove from the ship. "You try to take anything from this ship and I'll get a stick and knock your brains out!"

He added, "If I was here when McCarthy [a customs official] seized the ship I would have pumped him so full of lead it would have taken seven men to lift him, he would have been so heavy." Then directing his threats to Barbour, Dicks shouted, "If you try to hold me up, I'll make you a stranger in Heaven!"

The stand-off did not last long. The crew deserted Dicks, who sensing the determination of Barbour and his men, allowed them on board.

After securing the cargo on board and leaving several kegs of whiskey on deck to be unloaded the next day, Barbour assigned Frank Platts, one of the toughest preventive officers in the area, to supervisor several watchmen left on board.

Things seemed to be quite peaceful until Platts got a glimpse of Captain Dicks, decked off in his rubber boots and rubber clothes sneaking on board. By the time Platts made his way to Dicks, the captain was pouring himself a mug of rum from one of the kegs on deck.

Platts recognized Dicks and was well prepared for trouble. However, he was taken by surprise when Dicks downed his drink and quipped, "Have a drink yourself." Caught a little off-guard, Platts politely declined. He later recalled, "When he put down the mug he grabbed me by the shoulder with such a grip the like of which I had never experienced. I tell you this, I'll remember that grip the rest of my life."

He added, "For a brief moment it seemed like I was going to have to fight my way through this one. But he seemed to have had second thoughts and released his grip. As he walked away he said, "That's alright me son, you're only doing your duty."

Meanwhile, Captain Lillington was found not guilty by a jury. Other charges he was scheduled to face in Supreme Court regarding rum-running were withdrawn by the court because the Crown felt juries were sympathetic to rum-runners and would not convict them.

The charge of conspiracy was dropped due to lack of evidence. News of this was celebrated in Chicago, New York and Boston. For now, it was business as usual for the mob.

Chapter 5

Newfoundland Left A Big Imprint on the Prohibition Era

The end of World War I left many Newfoundlanders, particularly those whose livelihood depended on the sea, without a means of supporting themselves. As a result, more than a few sea captains and seamen, trained by the Royal Navy, turned to the lucrative bootlegging and rum-running business. Perhaps the best known of these was Captain Jack Randell, who even drew international attention in a standoff with the American Navy.

When World War I broke out, Jack Randell, a Newfoundland fishing captain, enlisted with the Royal Navy. By the time it ended, Randell was not only a decorated war hero but also held the rank of lieutenant commander. Newfoundlanders everywhere were proud of their war heroes, and he was among the most respected and admired.

Life after the war was not kind to Randell, who struggled to make a living in the fishery. He was working hard, but times were tough. "I was barely making a living," he often told friends. Things were about to take a dramatic turn in Randell's life when he encountered the gangster Big Jamie Clarke in New York.

Prohibition had just become law in the United States and gangsters across the country were having problems keeping up with supplying bootleggers and speakeasies with contraband liquor. Big Jamie and Randell held several meetings before the gangster offered him a deal he couldn't resist!

"You keep me supplied with contraband liquor and I'll get you your own vessel. You'll be in charge completely. Hire whoever you want and arrange your own supplies. There's big money to be made, Jack," Big Jamie told him, as though Jack was not already well aware of this. In fact, it was on his mind when he arrived in New York. Captain Randell didn't need time to think about the offer. "Let's go, I'm in," he answered.

Big Jamie was anxious to get underway, and the two of them headed to Lunenburg, Nova Scotia, where the gangster purchased a schooner called *I'm Alone*. From that day forward, the sole purpose of the vessel was to bring illegal whiskey from St. Pierre and the British Honduras to Big Jamie, outside the twelve-mile limit, off the coast of Louisiana.

Big Jamie paid $18,000 for the impressive looking *I'm Alone*. It weighed ninety tons, and measured 125 feet long and twenty-seven feet wide. The schooner was equipped with a 100hp diesel engine.

Even in his newly chosen career as a rum-runner for the mob, Captain Randell was the most daring, daunting and resourceful of the rum-runners. These qualities and more contributed to Randell becoming internationally known in one of the most famous incidents on the high seas to occur during Prohibition.

Working With the Mob

The two worked out a system to protect the operation from the Coast Guard and pirates. When the time came for the first run, the men took a bundle of fifteen U.S. bills each, with the middle bill torn in half and each half-bill was placed in the middle of each bundle. The serial number on the half-bill became the password used to identify participants in the scheme.

When time came to go into business, Randell was well aware that the Coast Guard had no jurisdiction in international waters, and staying outside that limit was his priority.

Rum-running was not all work for Randell, who between trips was often entertained by the mobsters. He was always ready for an invitation to socialize and took along an impressive wardrobe. This included a tuxedo, dinner jacket, six dress shirts, twelve dress collars, eighteen pairs of silk socks, several pairs of black leather shoes and a top hat.

Captain Randell provided an invaluable service to American gangsters during the Prohibition years. In doing so, he became a legendary figure in both Canada and the United States. One of his acts of bravado on the high seas, while transporting his cargoes of rum to their targets, even made international headlines. However, prior to his new career as a rum-runner, Randell had an outstanding background.

Pre-Rum-running Life

Captain Randell was born in 1879 in Port Rexton, then known as Ship Cove. His love for sea adventure led him to join the Royal Navy at the age of twenty and he was shipped out to South Africa to fight in the Boer War.

During that war, Randell was transferred to the Canadian Army where he served as an artilleryman with the Canadian Field Artillery. Although fellow soldiers were happy when they were pulled out of Africa, Randell volunteered to become a scout with Howard's Canadian Scouts, and served in the war until it ended. His courage did not go unnoticed. Upon returning to Newfoundland, he was presented with several medals for courage in battle by the Duchess of York and her husband, who later became King George V of England. By the time he reached the age of twenty-eight, he had earned his deep water master's ticket for any tonnage vessel on any ocean, steam or sail.

He Returned to Africa

Captain Randell was a rough and ready John Wayne-type of individual, who even fought professional fighters when visiting ports to raise money to purchase food. Widespread malaria and black water fever failed to discourage him from accepting an assignment on a dredger operating on Africa's west coast.

His abilities and fearlessness became so well-known that the British military often called upon him to deliver vessels all over the world. Randell became a favourite choice of Lloyd's of London for special assignments, after saving them thousands of dollars by salvaging a grounded dredger.

Involved in Espionage

His good relationship with the British led to him being appointed to deliver a new dredger to imperial Russia. This project brought him into German-Russian espionage. A German agent had stolen the blueprints of a Russian Naval base and was on his way out of the country on Randell's boat, carrying with him top secret documents.

The agent might have succeeded had Randell not out-manoeuvred him. Randell, after sending for Russian authorities, used his powerful social skills to stall the escaping spy. He drew the German into a conversation that led to a, "… see who can outdrink who," type of encounter. In order to stall the spy he boasted, "I can drink any man under the table." The spy couldn't resist.

While the two matched each other for drink, the Russian intelligence officers swept in and apprehended the German, red-handed with the stolen documents. The Russians were grateful, and the British earned themselves a favour because of the outcome of Randell's quick thinking.

He Goes to World War I

Shortly after World War I broke out, Randell found himself in the thick of the action; he skippered armed trawlers, minesweepers and sub-chasers. His performance in that war earned him a Distinguished Service Cross from King George V and the unofficial title, "Pirate of the Grand Fleet." Randell was also awarded The Croix de Guerre for his part in a battle with a German U-boat. Jack Randell retired from the Royal Navy as a lieutenant commander. In addition to his war experiences, he even skippered an Arctic expedition.

The difficult financial times that followed the war in Newfoundland pushed him towards becoming one of the most admired names among Prohibition's top rum-runners, and his success enriched many an American gangster. He was just the sort of man the New Yorkers wanted in their operation.[1]

First Encounter

The first encounter between the *I'm Alone* and the U.S. Coast Guard occurred during a delivery of whiskey from St. Pierre to Big Jamie, off the Louisiana coast. The *I'm Alone* arrived at night at the rendezvous point, and after the passwords were confirmed, Big Jamie began unloading the whiskey into his motor boat. He was successful in landing one load ashore, and had returned for a second load when, seemingly out of nowhere, the U.S. Coast Guard swept in to make an arrest.

Big Jamie quickly doused his cargo with gasoline, dumped it overboard and used a flare gun to set it afire. While the Coast Guard was distracted by Big Jamie, Captain Randell made a successful escape and chalked up the incident as part of the risk involved in his new profession. He was not deterred by it in the least.

1 *The Evening Telegram.* April 1929.

On March 20, 1929, Captain Randell was pursued by the Coast Guard cutter *Walcott*. Unarmed, the captain of the *Walcott* went on board the *I'm Alone* and informed Randell that he was operating illegally, and ordered him to surrender.

Randell claimed he was in international waters and the Coast Guard had no jurisdiction to challenge him. The captain returned to his ship and, after a short delay, sent several shots across the bow of the *I'm Alone*. When the Coast Guard gun jammed, Randell used the opportunity to escape. "See you in hell!" he shouted to the Coast Guard captain as he sped away.

The *Walcott* followed close behind. Gunfire from the cutter during the chase struck Randell in the leg. Serious injury did not result because only rubber bullets were used. By this time the cutter *Dexter* had caught up with the *Walcott* and joined in the chase.

What happened next sparked an international controversy that made newspaper headlines across Canada and the United States. The chase continued into the next day. When the Coast Guard caught up with Randell, the captain of the *Dexter* used a megaphone to order Randell to "Heave to!"

Once again, Captain Randell boisterously replied, "You can't touch us, we are in international waters. The Coast Guard has no jurisdiction out here!"

The *Dexter* responded by firing a volley of shots across the bow of the *I'm Alone* and, when it refused to stop, launched an all-out attack on the rum-runners. Real bullets ripped apart the sails of the schooner damaging it to the extent that Captain Randell ordered the crew to the lifeboats. Randell remained on board until the last minute. When the schooner nose-dived into the ocean, he jumped into the water, and was rescued by the Americans. One crewman of the schooner drowned during the confrontation.

Once on board the *Dexter*, the survivors were arrested, but treated well. They were given warm clothing, hot coffee and food. Following this, they were taken to New Orleans and put in jail. When arraigned in court, Randell insisted they were 200 miles off the U.S. coast when arrested, and there was no justification for the arrest.

For six years the case lingered in American courts, which angered the Canadian government. It ended in favour of the rum-runners. Because the *I'm Alone* was a Canadian-registered vessel, the American government extended an apology to Canada and paid the Canadian government $25,000. A total of $25,666.50 in compensation was paid to the crew of the *I'm Alone*. Captain Randell received $7,906, the family of the man who drowned received $10,000, and the remaining crewmembers divided the remainder among them.[2]

Rum-runners Kidnap Police

In the dying days of American Prohibition, rum-running along Rum Row became treacherous. The competition among gangsters in the United States was fierce and spilled over along the coastal areas, which had a very high traffic of ships involved in the trade. This period had the highest number of incidents involving gunfire, violence and piracy during the entire Prohibition era. The daring story of the *Kromhout* went one better. In addition to gunfire, the rum-running crew kidnapped the R.C.M.P. officers who boarded the vessel to seize it and arrest the crew.

The *Kromhout* episode was so sensational that it attracted media attention from all over North America. Captain Ross Mason, part owner of the ship, was a tough sea captain and an experienced rum-runner. The *Kromhout* was a Canadian-registered vessel on a delivery trip from St. Pierre when it caught the attention of the R.C.M.P. cutter *Stumble Inn*, seven miles off the coast at Cape Breton Island. As a Canadian-

2 This story is based on information in *Prohibition and St. Pierre*, Jean P. Andrieux, 1983.
"The Sinking of the *I'm Alone*", Janice Patton, 1973. *The Evening Telegram* and the *Daily News*, St. John's, NL. March-October 1929.

registered ship, the police had the legal right to board and inspect it inside the twelve-mile limit.

It was a cold, dark morning during December 1933, when the police boat attempted a boarding. To their surprise, Captain Mason had seen them approach and fled. *The Stumble Inn* swung into full speed and gave chase, firing "bow chasers" until Captain Mason brought his vessel to a stop. A prize crew was sent to board and take possession of the rum-running vessel. Captain Mason vehemently opposed this action and confidently insisted, "I'm outside the twelve-mile limit, and you can't touch me."

The police officer, equally as bold responded, "We are placing the vessel, captain and crew under arrest."

Once the seventy-foot-long tow line was secured, the course was set for North Sydney, with the rum-runner in tow. The captain of the police vessel was in disbelief when the *Kromhout* suddenly turned around and sped off towards the open sea. He didn't hesitate in his reaction as he shouted orders to give chase.

However, the gangsters were escaping with four police officers still on board, a fact which discouraged him from firing shots over its bow. Instead, he continued the chase while alerting all ships in the area of the unfolding drama.

Captain Mason had regained control of his vessel by taking advantage of a sudden storm that hit the area. He instructed his crew to stage a fight to distract the police officers. It worked. When the police came below deck to break up the racket, they were overpowered by Mason and his men. Mason then went to the wheel and wrestled control from the fourth and last police officer. He then cut the tow line and attempted to escape.

It was not long after the messages went out, that all available police craft were joining in the search. Eventually, police caught up with Captain Mason and reclaimed the vessel in addition to arresting Mason and crew.

The Crown brought three charges under Section 207 of the Customs Act relating to, "Hovering in territorial waters with a contraband cargo."

The trial was well covered by the media, and Mason was found guilty and sentenced to three years in Dorchester Penitentiary for each of the three counts: theft of his own ship, theft of its liquor cargo and resisting a police officer. The sentences ran concurrently. Captain Mason served every day of his sentence. However, he could never understand how any court could convict him of stealing his own ship.

A few years later, the Churchill brothers of Bay Roberts were looking to purchase a new schooner and turned to Nova Scotia to find one. Two of the brothers, Max and Bill, found a suitable one at Halifax Harbour and were delighted to purchase it. It turned out to be the *Kromhout*. The vessel served them well until 1965, when they sold it to Fishery Products. In 1968, she was declared unfit for service and tied up at Trinity where, a few years later, she sank.

Newfoundland Moonshiners

Chicago, New York and Boston were not the only hot spots during the Prohibition years. There were many stills operating throughout Newfoundland to supply the local market with illegal booze. The most notorious case of moonshining took place on Flat Islands, Bonavista Bay. When police attempted to break up the operation, an all-out war nearly erupted.

To end the conflict, authorities had to call in a British warship, scores of marines and a squad of hefty cops from the St. John's.

This epic story in our criminal history began in 1919, when police in St. John's received reliable reports that some people on Flat Islands were illegally brewing intoxicants and distributing them indiscriminately. Authorities sent Constable

John Summers to investigate the report and in Greenspond he was joined by another constable.

The two proceeded to Flat Islands. On Coward Island, near Flat Island, they went ashore and searched five houses, but failed to turn up any evidence of moonshining. As they arrived at Flat Island, they encountered three motorboats carrying fifty men. Summers, an experienced police officer, took control of the situation. He stood up in the boat, identified himself, and began asking questions about the stills.

The police were told blatantly by the men to leave the area or be tossed into the water. Summers sensed they meant business and decided to avoid a confrontation at that time and returned to Greenspond. The moonshiners thought there would be no further threat from the man from St. John's. However, back in Greenspond, Summers telegraphed Police Inspector C.H. Hutchings. The inspector sent ten men to help Summers complete his investigation and enforce the law.

A more confident Summers led the police unit to Flat Island, hoping to arrest the group leaders. When word spread that the police were back, people went to their homes and returned to the wharf armed with guns and ammunition.

They hid behind rocks and boulders and warned the police to leave or, "...be blown to hell." Outnumbered by nearly 200 angry and armed people, Summers once again retreated. Once more, he returned to Greenspond to seek help. He sent a second telegraph to the police inspector in St. John's pleading for more help. Inspector Hutchings was determined that the law be obeyed on Flat Island, and felt this would require extraordinary measures.

He called upon the HMS *Cornwall*, which was visiting St. John's port, and requested that its crew of British marines go assist his men in Greenspond.

The *Cornwall* picked up Summers and his men at Greenspond and launched a military assault on Flat Island, which prompted one elder there to comment, "...the likes of it has never been seen around these parts before."

By this time, most of the Flat Island men were away prosecuting the Labrador fishery. The remaining men offered no resistance and the assault team arrested seven ringleaders. A woman watching the spectacle became hysterical because she believed the marines were going to shoot her husband, one of the men who had been arrested. Another seven men, returning from the Labrador fishery, were arrested and were brought with the others to St. John's for trial.

Summers got his way. With the assistance of the Navy, he showed the Flat Islands fishermen that they must respect those who enforce the law. However, amid the confusion and frustration of making the arrests, the police failed to gather evidence needed for the trial. The case went through a series of delays and the Flat Islanders returned home and resumed their moonshining activities.

The HMS *Cornwall* carried an *Evening Telegram* reporter in its assault on Flat Island. He was Joey Smallwood, who later led Newfoundland into Confederation and became the province's first premier.

Newfoundland Prime Minister and Flat Island Moonshiners

Hollis Walker stated:

Prohibition left few areas of politics untouched in some way, but no single element had its future more adversely affected than the Union movement. The reason was simple: among the leading Prohibitionists was William Coaker. A total abstainer himself and long an active combatant in the fight against 'demon rum,' when the opportunity arose to strike it what he thought would be mortal blow, he unhesitatingly lent his great authority and the Union newspaper 'to the anti-cause.'[3]

An intriguing aspect of this story involved Sir Richard Squires. He represented the Flat Island moonshiners when they first appeared in court. The courts kept delaying the case, and once Squires became prime minister the case disappeared. There was political speculation that this was part of a deal made by Squires to gain the political support of Sir William Coaker, whose union members included the accused fishermen.

Many Newfoundland merchants were pleased when Prohibition was brought to an end by the administration which succeeded Squires. Colonial Secretary J.R. Bennett, co-owner of the Bennett Brewing Company, the largest brewery in St. John's, was nearing bankruptcy due to Prohibition, when his party won a general election.

One of his first actions was to bring legislation that ended Prohibition. With the sale of liquor wide open again, Bennett's company prospered. Bennett was not the only minister to blatantly advance his own personal interests.

Historian S.J.R. Noel commented:

The new Prime Minister Walter Monroe had done nothing to improve the administration over that of the defeated party. So, far from being enemies of the old system, they were its quintessential products; their habits of political thought and behaviour had been moulded by it; under it, and indeed to a large degree because of it, they had materially prospered and risen to positions of political power. It is hardly surprising, therefore, that they should have shown neither the will nor the imagination to carry out substantial alterations.[4]

3 The Hollis Walker Commission
4   Noel, S.J.R. *Politics in Newfoundland.* University of Toronto Press.1971. pp180.

Chapter 6

Prohibition Starts Bootlegging Boom

B efore Newfoundland became the mobster's Jewel of the Atlantic, it struggled under its own Prohibition, which was enacted on January 1, 1917 and was repealed in 1924. The following chapters look at the era of Prohibition in Newfoundland, leading up to the colony becoming a major rum-running port for mobsters during American Prohibition.

During the early nineteenth century, the taverns or public houses, as they were also called, were actually the centres of social enjoyment. St. John's and adjacent areas had a total of thirty-three such taverns. William Best boasted of owning the sign of The Bunch of Grapes, located at Bully's Farm, on the north side of Quidi Vidi Pond. Along the Lower Path (Water Street) were: Cornelius Mark's London Tavern, John Cahill's Tar for All Weathers, Edward Angel's Britannia and John Widdecombe's Rose and Crown.

The London Tavern was the most exclusive, and was popular among city merchants and visiting naval officers.It was also where some Regatta committee meetings were held. It featured billiard tables and regularly held elegant dinners and dances. Songs that were popular at the time, and were likely heard at these events, include: "Heart of Oak," "Rule Britannia," "Barbara Allan," "Phillida Flouts Me," "Bonnie Dundee," and "Prince Charlie."

An amazing quantity of spirits was consumed for the small population of 20,000 people. Imports alone accounted for 220,000 gallons, or eleven gallons per head, annually for everyone in Newfoundland. This amount did not include brandy, gin, wine, beer and cider, which accounted for the consumption of additional five or six gallons annually.

H.M. Mosdell, editor of the *Royal Gazette*, 1907, appropriately noted:

> Surely there were giants in the earth in those days. These taverns must have been interesting places. Sailors from war ships, soldiers and marines, hobnobbed with merchant seamen, fishermen and the wondering Irish youngster, and each had his tale of marvellous adventures. Some of the navy men had doubtless, been with Nelsen at Copenhagen or the Nile or had convoyed ships through thrilling adventure.[1]

The birth of the temperance movement in Newfoundland had its origins on October 2, 1841, at the St. Mary's Roman Catholic Church, perhaps better known as the Old Chapel on Henry Street, and in more recent times as the Star of the Sea Hall in St. John's.

Bishop Michael Anthony O'Donnell, whom many modern-day Catholic Newfoundlanders believe would be a suitable candidate for ordination to sainthood, was alarmed over the prolific number of taverns in the town and the devastating affect it was having on families and the community. At Sunday Mass October 2nd, he plunged into the issue with force and inspiration to denounce, "...the evils of drink." He ended his sermon with the announcement that he was forming a temperance movement which "...will be open to all."

The following month, a Father Murphy in Ferryland fuelled the new movement, and speaking in his distinctively strong Irish brogue proceeded to mesmerize the congregation by denouncing the demon drink, and in a dramatic move at the

1 Mosdell, H.M. *When Was That?* 1923.

end of Mass stood at the foot of the altar and took the pledge. Six hundred parishioners followed him.

Protestants and Catholics flocked to the temperance movement, however, Catholics swore off the use of liquor by taking an oath while the Protestants substituted tea for liquor.

The first annual Temperance Day parade, which the public dubbed "The Teetotal Procession," was held on January 6, 1843. In those days, any kind of public demonstration attracted notice in small town St. John's, the teetotallers were an exceptional attraction.

Several bands led the parade, including the Garrison Band and two amateur bands, accompanied by a sprinkling of fiddlers, drummers and tin-whistles. The farmers of the town were well represented. One hundred of them riding on horseback in double file marched proudly behind the military band. At the head of the procession, was a three-man contingent carrying a large portrait of Queen Victoria. All along the way, people stepped forward to join the marchers and followed them up Cochrane Street and onto Government House grounds, where they were addressed by the Newfoundland governor.

The movement grew so rapidly that by the end of 1844, the Total Abstinence (TA) Society had gathered 10,000 pledges and the consumption of tea in town had skyrocketed.

The temperance movement was strengthened in 1843, when the Church of England Temperance Society held a temperance festival at a site off King's Bridge Road called the Old Factory. A summer temperance festival followed that same year at Cherry Gardens on Waterford Bridge Road, also known as the Road to Petty Harbour. In 1850, the Congregational Hall, at the foot of Victoria Street, became Temperance Hall.

Throughout the 1850s, the temperance movement became entrenched in St. John's. In 1858, William McGrath, a blacksmith who operated a forge on the western corner of the Hill O'Chips and Water Street, launched the Total Abstinence and Benefit Society, which became known as the teetotalers. McGrath called an open air public meeting in a large field, west of his building, which had a huge flat rock in the middle that he used as a pulpit to address the gathering.

In 1859, the Teetotalers' Band led the official parade to open a new street in town, which was appropriately called Temperance Street. In succeeding years, the temperance group moved its headquarters from Factory Lane to St. Patrick's Schoolroom at Riverhead, in the west end of St. John's, the Cathedral Fire Brigade Hall and finally the organization was able to purchase its own building at the corner of Bell Street and Duckworth Street in 1873. The Great Fire of 1892, which destroyed most of St. John's, destroyed this building.

On June 29, 1893, the corner stone was laid for a new hall, which when completed stood three stories high, 106 feet long and sixty-five feet wide. The Total Abstinence Society occupied the first floor, the society's club rooms were on the second floor, and on the third floor was a new theatre named the Capitol Theatre.

Prohibition Becomes Law in Newfoundland

By the beginning of the twentieth century, the abuse of alcohol had become a major problem in the British colonies, including Newfoundland, and was causing serious injury to the moral, social and industrial welfare of its people. The British government considered it serious enough to deem it, "... a social peril and a national menace."[2]

There was a belief that Prohibition would decrease crime, instead, when it came, it attracted a fair number of Newfoundlanders into the rum-running operations, in addition to moonshining and bootlegging.

2 The Royal Commission on the Liquor Traffic: The Facts of the Case. The Dominion Alliance for the Total Suppression of the Liquor Traffic. Toronto, 1896.p8

None of the social changes that took place throughout Newfoundland during World War I were as powerful and influential on the country as was the introduction of Prohibition in 1917. Author S.J.R. Noel explained:

> Even St. John's known well for its number and variety of taverns, officially became 'dry.' ...The actual result of course, was to initiate a virtually uncontrollable traffic in the illegal importation, manufacture, and sale of liquor; prohibition ensured that the bootlegger, rather than the publican shared in the fruits of prosperity. It also had far-reaching political consequences.[3]

Yet, it was mostly the fishermen and working men, who were small-time operators in the schemes to bootleg, who became easy targets for justice. Knowledge of the involvement of prominent politicians and businessmen, who even benefited from American and Canadian Prohibition, has largely been lost to history. The R.C.M.P. and a Royal Commission investigation did expose a great deal about a conspiracy in operation but none were convicted. The roots of temperance groups and the discontent that led to Prohibition began with Newfoundlanders' thirst for Demerara rum.

Origins of Rum in Newfoundland

Screech rum, popularized as Newfoundland rum, and part of our Newfoundland culture, has origins in the seventeenth century when schooners from St. John's delivered fish to the West Indies. Part of the payment made to them for their cargoes was in rum. Widespread consumption of the drink developed in St. John's and led to many an uproar among the

---

3 Noel, S. J. R. , *Politics in Newfoundland*, University of Toronto Press , p132

town's summer population. The product was dubbed Screech, and led to the development and growth of strong temperance movements.

The actual sale of rum in Newfoundland can be traced back to Sir David Karce of Ferryland in 1640. Karce operated a profitable tavern in his home, and his customers included shipmasters, their crews, and anyone else who came along.

The first taverns appeared in St. John's in 1680 and catered to the summer fishery crowd. By 1801, the town had thirty-six licensed taverns. These caused so much trouble in such a short period of time that twelve licences were suspended. Later, to obtain a licence the applicant was required to provide the services of a police constable or bobby for six months without pay.[4]

An interesting aspect of the history of Newfoundland Screech is that it led to a law being passed that outlawed the sale of rum, and forced all liquor outlets to close on Election Day. Previously, drinking on Election Day caused voters to interrupt and interfere with the voting process, intimidate politicians, riot and destroy properties. Several deaths even occurred.

Temperance movements became so strong that they influenced the Newfoundland government to introduce the Prohibition Act on January 1, 1917. For a brief period, Newfoundland was, "As dry as a bone!" But not for long.

An *Evening Telegram* editorial in August 1917 stated:

Newfoundland today enters a new era that will be fraught with increased prosperity to her people because money that was wasted on liquor will be diverted to provide the comforts and   necessities of life.[5]

4 Smallwood Joseph R. *Book of Newfoundland.* Vol. 5. article by J. Withers.
5 Moakler, Leo. "Screech and Prohibition: 1640-1924." *Newfoundland Ancestor,* Fall 1991, Vol. 7(3) pp104-107

Leo Moakler retrospectively claimed, "The abuses of former times were only a picnic to the chaos that followed."[6] Still, there was genuine concern that one of Newfoundland's prized exports could be threatened by Prohibition.

Townies and Baymen Divided in Referendum

The Prohibition referendum battle was fought between two groups – those in favour, the pros, and those against, the antis. When it was finally settled, one wag said, "If fat back was brains, neither side would have enough to fry a touton." If all those against Prohibition had gotten out to vote there would not have been a Prohibition. The pro-side won the referendum despite their devious plan.

Both sides conducted misleading campaigns. St. John's businessmen were convinced that a majority vote was absolutely essential to Prohibition becoming law. Based on this conviction, they developed a strategy aimed at discouraging people from voting on referendum day. The aim was simple — if less than a majority of the voting population of Newfoundland voted in the Prohibition referendum, then government could not legislate it.

The business community sent out workers to put up posters in all saloons and licensed premises which read, "If you Don't want Prohibition — Don't vote." So those who enjoyed a drink and were vehemently opposed to Prohibition paid heed to the message, and on polling day stayed in the taverns and "drank 'er up" instead of casting a ballot.

The License Dealers Association had not factored in the distrust the baymen held towards townies. Politically, the slogan, "St. John's gets everything," was persuasive during elections in turning the outports against St. John's. This perception convinced them that by voting for Prohibition,

6 Ibid

they would stop the townies from being able to purchase rum, while they could pick up puncheons to bring back to the bays.

When outport voters realized this, they saw an opportunity to pull a fast one on the townies. They encouraged friends and neighbours to vote for Prohibition by telling them, "We'll vote for Prohibition. The townie won't be able to get a sniff of rum and we'll be free to buy our own supplies of rum."

When spring came and the baymen poured into St. John's, they realized they had outsmarted themselves. Prohibition had passed, because it required the majority of only the total number of votes cast and most ballots were cast in the outports. It was the stupidity of the License Dealers Association along with the dishonest propaganda circulated by the pros that gave the teetotallers their victory. The long drought began.[7]

Survival of Port Wine Threatened

The introduction of Prohibition nearly killed the Newfoundland port wine industry. Writers have described Newfoundland's port wine as, "...one of the romances of the wine industry of the world — the finest known to man." This glowing description of our port wine doesn't recognize that it is only ripened in Newfoundland and not produced here.

Newfoundland fish was exported to Portugal year round, and when returning home these vessels carried a cargo of multiple items, including port wine made in Iberia. There was nothing unusual about this wine at first. It was sold in public houses in St. John's and popular among the merchants. Then consumers began noticing that quantities stored here for a long time had a distinctively superior taste from the port wine consumed soon after arrival.

Historian H.F. Shortis wrote:

7 Prohibition Vote: For Prohibition: 24,965, Against Prohibition: 5,348 – *Royal Gazette* St. John's, November 30, 1915. Over fifty percent did not vote, and Prohibition came into effect on January 1, 1917.

After remaining here some time, it had improved in quality and possessed properties which, in its original condition were unknown. The hard-drinking Devonshire fishers, who ruled supreme in our Colony in those days, were loud in their satisfaction at the change, and although they were unaware as whether the transformation was effected by the voyage or the climate, or by both, they were prompt to avail themselves of the fact and import still larger quantities.[8]

The main consumers of this wine were Devonshire fishermen who were the first to notice the improved quality of the imported wine. They had no idea if the enhanced quality resulted during the Atlantic crossing or if it was from the Newfoundland climate. Perhaps it was both, some thought. Whatever the cause, they began importing it in much larger quantities. Over a period of a few years, the demand for port wine grew in England due to efforts made by the Devonshire fish merchants with branches in St. John's.

In time, the popularity of port wine, aged in Newfoundland, spread throughout Europe, the American colonies and Canada. Shortis observed, "In these cases a goodly cliental with cultivated tastes had become initiated to the merits of the vintage and learned to appreciate its excellent qualities."[9]

The Newman family of merchants built large vaults in St. John's, which were used to age the wine. Using scientific principles known at the time, they developed a very high quality of port wine which has remained popular to this day. One of their vaults was built on the corner of Springdale and Water streets, near the western corner. The second was in the east end of St. John's, on Water Street near Prescott Street. This was exposed during the construction of Harbour Drive,

8 H.F. Shortis, "A Unique Industry May be Killed by Recent Prohibition Act." Papers at Centre Newfoundland Studies
9 Ibid

on the portion which connected it to Water Street. City council records of the 1930s mentioned that Councillor Mullally was in charge of those vaults at that time. The British military purchased their own wine supplies and sent it to St. John's to be ripened. Once Prohibition entered the picture, a variety of substitutes found their way into the illegal markets.

Scripts and Dope

A term that originated during Prohibition to describe a legal way to obtain illegal liquor was "the scripts." These were actually prescriptions issued by family doctors to those patients who required alcohol for a multitude of medicinal purposes. The legislation permitted doctors to issue scripts for eight ounces of alcohol daily, providing the doctor felt it was necessary.

This practice led to outrageous abuse of scripts with certain favoured imbibers walking away from the controllers, as the bonded warehouses storing the liquor were called.

By August, 1917, government found it necessary to amend the Prohibition Act, in particular, to cover the loophole caused by scripts. The success of this move was reflected in the abrupt decline of the number of drunks being arrested. Scripts were also part of Prohibition laws in Canada and the United States.

In searching for a way of getting around the law, imbibers came up with a very clever alternative. In doing so, a new word was introduced into Prohibition culture right across North America. It was "dope." Its meaning was in no way similar to the meaning of dope in today's world. Dope then was not a chemical product, it was entirely in liquid form and easily available at the corner grocery stores. After all, there were many items not covered by law that had some alcohol content within its mixture. Products like tonics, lotions and cooking additives were given close scrutiny before their sales suddenly boomed. Just about any liquid containing alcohol was sought.

Among the choices were: beef-iron and wine, Bay rum, Florida water, Sheriff's extract of vanilla, Royal extract of lemon, Jamaica ginger and norvaline. These were used by individuals to make their own brew.

Most of the drunk and disorderly convictions arose from the consumption of dope. This is supported by the police records of arrests for drunk and disorderly conduct. The numbers are as follows:

1917: 87 arrests
1918: 95 arrests
1919: 228 arrests
1920: 276 arrests

The police records from 1917-1918 did not record the number of drunks as a result of dope, but did in 1920. Out of 228 arrests in 1919, 198 were because of dope. Out of 276 cases in 1920, 198 were dope related. In 1919, by far, the majority of arrests were due to the abuse of dope. One method of attacking this problem was blacklisting many essences as well as increasing police activities. These efforts had partial success, but smuggled liquor and liquor obtained on scripts were factors.[10]

On August 14, 1920, government stepped in, pressured by the teetotalers, and banned these products (dope). The new law had a loophole that was detected almost immediately. It failed to specify the individual products.

Just as rapidly, there was a boom among the grocery stores in sales of Hall's Balsam of Honey and Brown's Bronchial of Elixir. After the government discovered this and outlawed it on February 10, 1921, some turned to drinking shoe polish mixed with water. Others downed wood alcohol, a deadly

10 Baker, Melvin. *Prohibition Plebiscite.*

brew. A beverage called Royal Household, which sold for $1.50 a bottle contained a mixture of 16.2 percent alcohol and a measure of diethlypalate.[11]

The bootleggers hid illegal alcohol and dope in soft drink bottles, essence of vanilla bottles and even tobacco cans. The smart bootlegger did not store his liquor in his own home. Usually, it was hid at a friend's house, or on a shop shelf concealed as an everyday consumer product. When the use of dope declined it was replaced by homemade alcohol, which was known as moonshine.

In St. Pierre the manufacturing, storage and export of liquor was not illegal. However, in Newfoundland bootleggers began setting up their own stills to get in on the illegal trade. When Newfoundland police began locating these stills and arresting the bootleggers involved, they had to use a cell in the lock-up to store the moonshine.

Premises selling the illegal hop beer became known as shebeens, and on the mainland were called blind pigs. A glass of hop beer was sold for 0.05 cents. The fine for operating a shebeen was nominal and was not a deterrent for bootleggers. One newspaper letter noted, "The bold and brazen flouting of the law during Prohibition years was unprecedented in the history of the country."

Fishermen from Newfoundland went to St. Pierre and lived on their boats in the harbour. They kept wood from crates and brought it home to build houses similar to those at St. Pierre at the time.

Leo Moakler said that the most ingenious of the containers used by the bootlegger was, "The breast-plate. Made of metal it could hold a gallon of spirits. It was fashioned in such a way that it could be moulded to the body beneath the waistcoat without being noticeable on the wearer."[12]

11 Ibid
12 Moakler, Leo. *The Newfoundland Ancestor.* p107

Newfoundlanders Sought Liquor from St. Pierre

Historian Andrieux revealed that Newfoundlanders concluded business with St. Pierre during the Newfoundland Prohibition. He stated:

> There had always been alcoholic beverages at St. Pierre, the traditional products of the motherland as well as rum from the French Caribbean islands. A thriving barter trade grew between St. Pierre and Newfoundland ports. Newfoundlanders would supply firewood (billets) scallops, mussels, clams and game birds, all in short supply at St. Pierre. The St. Pierrais had plenty of wine and liquor to trade in return.
>
> On St. Pierre, the merchants were well aware that U.S. Prohibition, by then in effect, could transform the island into a transhipment port from where liquor could be forwarded to the U.S. and also Canada.[13]

That is just what happened when a decree on July 8, 1919, which outlawed the importation of sugar, molasses and alcohol from foreign sources to save foreign exchange, was lifted on April 18, 1922. Two years later, Prohibition ended in Newfoundland and it also became a transhipment port.

Beer and Breweries in Newfoundland

During the initial days of fishermen and settlers coming to Newfoundland, "Beer was commonly used as an alternative to water. As a result beer became a staple of fishermen and early colonists starting with John Guy at Cupids." At the end of 1611, Guy recorded in his inventory of provisions, "fourteen pipes of beer." According to the *Encyclopaedia of*

13 Andrieux, Jean Pierre. *Over the Side.* p17

81

Newfoundland, a note for required provisions for a voyage to Newfoundland dated, August 3, 1613, recommended fifty hogsheds of beer for the voyage.

In 1622, Sir Richard Whitbourne brought twenty-six tons of beer to Newfoundland. Sir William Vaughan told all who would listen, that strong liquor was unhealthy in cold climates and recommended barley and root beer.

It was almost 300 years later when Newfoundland got its first brewery. That was in 1802, when Alexander Caine was granted a permit to operate a malt beer brewery at Mundy's Brook, which feeds Mundy Pond in northern St. John's.[14]

Lindberg Brewing Company Limited

J. Lindberg, along with two unnamed partners, opened a brewery on Signal Hill in St. John's around 1877. His original partner was replaced by a man named Franklin. Lindberg's manufactured a wide selection of Bavarian beer, ales, stouts and aerated water.

In 1898, Lindberg introduced Jubilee and Klondike beers, and became the agent and bottler for Bass & Company ale and London Celebrated stout. At that time, Lindberg was the only producer of Bavarian ale in Newfoundland.

St. John's also had a small brewery called the Kavanagh Brewery located on Military Road. This brewery manufactured aerated water and confection drinks. This brewery operated into the 1930s.

Riverhead Brewery

Bennett Brewery was certainly not a fly-by-night operation. It had much history behind it by the time Prohibition crippled it. Charles Fox Bennett was operating: brewery, sawmill,

14 Smallwood, Joseph R., *Encyclopaedia of Newfoundland and Labrador*, , Vol I, Newfoundland Book Publishers

foundry, forge, flour mill and whiskey distillery at Riverhead, St. John's, as early as 1827. The brewery, then named the Riverhead Brewery, was made possible by the installation of a waterwheel in the western upper end of what is known today as Victoria Park. The wheel was fed by a dam built on Mullins River, which flowed down through the park from Mundy Pond. By the mid-twentieth century, the waterwheel area had been converted into a swimming hole.

In 1883, control of the brewery was passed to Edward W. Bennett, no relation to Charles Fox Bennett. Sharing in ownership at that time was John B. Ayre and George Ayre, and the business was named the E.W. Bennett & Co. While ownership had changed, the product remained the same. Bennett's was famous for its ale, porter, stout, cider, aerated water champagne, sasparilla, lemonade and raspberry nectar drinks.[15]

In 1845, it is a true story that John Grant and Thomas Walker drowned in a fermenting vat at the brewery. By the 1920s, a local wit added to it that, Grant refused rescue, claiming he was fine, "just foine!" He went down for the third time and became the second fatality in the vat that day.

In 1893, Newfoundland Brewery Ltd. moved to a new plant on the corner of Elizabeth Avenue and Rennies Mill River. The fire of 1892, followed by the bank crash of 1894, brought the brewery to a standstill. In 1900, they were in full operation again with new premises on Circular Road and produced: beer, porter and aerated water.

Early closing hours, brought about by the efforts of the temperance movement followed by Prohibition in 1917, hit the brewery industry hard. During Prohibition, this brewery produced near beer and aerated water. When Prohibition was repealed in 1924, they returned to the beer industry. At this time they introduced India Beer and India Pale Ale.

15 Ibid

John Bennett, friend of Sam Bronfman of Montreal and later Newfoundland's colonial secretary, took control of what was then called, Riverhead Brewery, located at 258-260 Water Street. John, Edward's brother, had the company incorporated with Sir Michael Cashin, R.J. Ryan, James O'Brien and Albert O'Reilly as partners. The brewery was renamed the Bennett Brewing Company.[16]

The brewery was prosperous until Prohibition was declared in 1917, forcing the shareholders to seriously consider liquidation. It narrowly avoided taking this action by turning to manufacturing the legally approved near beer, which was limited to two percent alcohol. In 1918, the Bennett Brewing Company was producing and distributing Haig ale and Haig stout, named after Field Marshall Earl Haig.

Bennett was instrumental in having Prohibition lifted, and his brewery returned to prosperity and growth. In 1924, he introduced Dominion ale, Dominion stout and Golden lager.

During the conspiracy trial of the "sixty-two," which included the Bronfman Brothers of Montreal, a Montreal brewery known as Dominion Breweries was implicated in the alleged conspiracy. The Bronfman's were not convicted of any crime during these trials, and were able to show certificates confirming that liquor exported by them was carried out according to Canada's custom laws.

Bavarian Brewing Company

In 1932, Garrett Brownrigg, owner of the Royal Aerated Water Company Limited manufacturer and bottler of Royal beverages (soft drinks), built a new brewing facility on Leslie Street in St. John's called the Bavarian Brewing Company Limited. Its first brewmaster was German-born

16 Ibid

84

Hans Schneider, who lived in an apartment on the premises. Schneider developed the popular products Jockey Club and Dark Munich. In 1937, the brewery added a soft drink operation to its plant and developed two ten-cent, near-beer lagers, Three Star and Pilsner.

Balance of World Power Influenced the End of Prohibition

When Responsible government collapsed and Commission of Government took over, Newfoundland became more responsive to British demands. Author Mark C. Hunter noted, "As a cross-jurisdictional issue, the general nature of Anglo-American relations influenced discussions on Maritime policing and Britain wanted greater help from Newfoundland to appease the United States." This was due to the change in balance of power which had shifted from Britain to the United States. Britain had become a debtor nation. According to Hunter, by 1923 Britain had to accept the responsibility of full repayment of its war debt, high interest rate, and the scaling down of its demands on former allies and Germany. It was in this atmosphere that Britain agreed to demands to help the United States in the policing of rum-running during Prohibition as part of new policy of cooperation.[17]

Members of the 1924 administration that repealed Prohibition included:

• Prime Minister and Minister of Education: Walter Monroe
• Colonial Secretary: J.R. Bennett
• Minister of Justice and Attorney General: W.J. Higgins
• Minister of Finance and Customs: Sir John Crosbie
• Minister of Posts and Telegraphs: W. Woodford

17 Hunter, Mark. *Changing the Flag: The Cloak of Newfoundland Registry for American Rumrunning, 1924-1934.* pp41-69

- Ministers without portfolio: A.B. Morine, MLC. M.S. Sullivan, R. Cramn, F. G. Bradley, J.J. Long.
- Outside cabinet: Minister of Agriculture and Mines, W.J. Walsh.

Chapter 7

Newfoundland's Biggest Bootlegger

One of several key players in the shadows of corruption and scandal surrounding Prime Minister Richard Squires in 1923 was John Meaney, whom the prime minister had appointed to the position of acting liquor controller for Newfoundland in 1920. Among his conditions of employment was that he be, "...expressly forbidden to receive any profits, brokerage or commission in connection with imported liquor." That's what the law said, but it was totally ignored by Meaney.

Meaney was a political supporter of Squires and had worked on the Squires-owned newspaper the *Daily Star*. When he accepted the position, he had been promised that, in time, he would be appointed controller of the Newfoundland Liquor Control (NLC). Until then, he was its top man with a political secret. He was bagman for Squires and his Liberal Reform Party.

Historian S.J.R Noel said, "Unenforceable laws are notorious causes of political corruption, especially where fortunes are to be made by their unhindered evasion." Prohibition became law in Newfoundland in 1917, and the Responsible government system, which was based on spoils, became a definitive example of Noel's observation. He elaborated:

> Poorly paid and insecure officials, politicians with an eye to the 'reward of office,' and those who had influence with politicians, suddenly found themselves exposed to, or able to find, temptations on a scale

previously unimaginable. And the richer the rewards the more deeply entrenched and resistant to reform the system itself became.[1]

A referendum on Prohibition was held in November, 1915, with fifty percent of eligible voters not voting. Prohibitionists won the referendum by a vote of 24,965 to 5,348. Prohibition became law in 1917[2], and the Meaney-run Newfoundland Liquor Control soon became known as the biggest bootlegging operation in Newfoundland. Meaney used his department to become the top distributor of liquor on the island, and much of the illegal income earned ended up in the business bank account of Sir Richard.

Upon his appointment, Meaney became responsible for the importation, sale and distribution of liquor into Newfoundland. Although he was under the supervision of the Board of Liquor Control, he totally ignored them and operated as the Liquor Czar of Newfoundland. Just as he ignored the board, the board ignored him, and never made any effort to monitor his activities. Because the Liquor Act contained a loophole, Meaney was able to operate his bootlegging scheme.

People with the right connections were able to obtain liquor through Meaney. The Liquor Czar held the authority to supply liquor for medical reasons, when requested with a doctor's prescription.[3] However, this was not the source of Meaney's bootleg income. That income was derived through his authority to supply liquor without scripts. And so he did! Through this matter he was able to divert large amounts of money to himself and Squires.

Meaney bestowed gifts of liquor to people and organizations without recording any payment or gratuity. In effect, the establishment in St. John's hardly knew that Prohibition was in effect. At least the flow of liquor did not

1 Noel, S.J.R. *Politics in Newfoundland.* University of Toronto Press. 1971.
2 *Royal Gazette,* November 30, 1919.
3 This practice was defined earlier as the scripts.

become a hardship for them. Neither did it deprive Squires supporters from quenching a thirst.

The house of cards began to collapse when the Hollis Walker Enquiry was set up to investigate allegations of corruption against Squires and others in his administration. The enquiry focused on bank accounts and financial records. All income, whether script or non-script, should have been deposited in the Newfoundland exchequer account. If that had been done, then any mistaken or illegal earnings would be detected during auditing. That was not done.

All income from script sales ended up in the Newfoundland exchequer account at the Bank of Montreal. Other income was kept under the control of Meaney, who did keep a special account but refrained from depositing all monies. Evidence later suggested that Squires may have been deliberately setting the wheels in motion to protect himself and, if necessary, to confuse investigators if the matter came under investigation. There was also room to suggest that he may have been a victim of circumstances.

In 1923, the administration of Prime Minister William Warren, who had succeeded Squires, set up the Hollis Walker Enquiry to investigate corruption in the Squires administration. Warren even personally prepared the evidence against his former boss. Responsible Government administrations were never really squeaky clean, and one administration accusing another of scandal had to tread lightly for fear of their own misdeeds and skeletons in the closet coming to light. Prime Minister Warren, aware of this, cautiously narrowed the enquiry's terms of reference.[4] There were areas of possible corruption that concerned the enquiry chairman, who was limited from investigating by these restrictions.

Squires was bothered by the enquiry from the start and even tried to intimidate his successor Prime Minister William Warren while the two were attending an imperial conference

4 Noel, S.J.R. *Politics in Newfoundland.* University of Toronto Press. P161.

in London. Warren recorded that Squires made every effort to embarrass and intimidate him into halting the investigation. Warren in a letter to one of his ministers wrote:

> He [Squires] has been circulating several stories about me, and, in particular, he poses as Leader of the Liberal Party, says that while he resigned his official position he is still the Leader of the Liberal Party, has told this to officials in the Colonial Office who do not believe him and he states that you [Halfyard] and Barnes deliberately left St. John's so that you would not sit at Council meeting with me at my final meeting before coming to the Conference because you were so disgusted with the way in which I was mismanaging matters.[5]

Hollis Walker was a distinguished British lawyer appointed to investigate the allegations of criminal conduct in the Squires administration. Walker was noted for his abilities as a cross-examiner who conducted relentless and painstaking research and investigation. Throughout the enquiry his impartiality and authority were never questioned. The events which became the target of the historic Hollis Walker Enquiry began when Squires was out of the country from August to December 1920, and Jean Miller was faced with the task of coming up with funds to keep the law offices and newspaper operating.

Jean Miller approached Meaney at the NLC requesting a loan for Squires which she, in turn, deposited in the Squires law firm bank account. This became a regular practice. Squires had loosely controlled his finances by depositing income from his law firm, the *Daily Star*, the Liberal Reform Party and monies from Meaney, all into his law firm account.

5 PANL-Warren Papers, September 28, 1923.

Walker had a difficult time determining just where the money was coming from. When Leslie R. Curtis became a partner in the firm, he told Squires that this practice of banking had to stop. During the Hollis Walker Enquiry, Meaney claimed he made similar loans to others but had no records to show any of such loans having been made. The audit of Meaney's books by Walker uncovered a very large shortage of funds estimated between $100,000 and $200,000. Meanwhile, all of the script sale money collected for liquor sales by Meaney were accounted for with the bank, but questionably non-script payments were not.

Before delving further into the allegations of corruption against Sir Richard Squires and members of his administration, I need to provide some background to this episode in Newfoundland history so the reader may understand the context under which it all happened.

The private and personal finances of Sir Richard Squires suffered between 1919 and 1923, after he became prime minister. He had a personal account at the Canadian Bank of Commerce and his business account at the Bank of Nova Scotia. Neither account was in great shape. His political obligations kept him away from his law firm, which he left subordinates to operate.

The illness of colleagues in government often required him to fill in and cover their duties, was also a contributing factor. His partnership with Alexander Winter, son of Sir James Winter, a former prime minister of Newfoundland, was dissolved in 1920 and Squires left the management of his office to Miss Miller. Political obligations caused him to neglect his law firm altogether, and he would go for weeks without contacting the office or checking his office books. On the few occasions in which he did visit the firm, he was always in a rush.

He had to depend a great deal on Miss Miller and placed much trust in her abilities. She was a practicing accountant before being hired by Sir Richard in September, 1916, for the position of office manager. During the Squires-Winters partnership, Miller had signing authority for both men. She was also given power of attorney, enabling her to draw, accept or endorse bills, promissory notes and cheques in their names. Her authority included the power to pay or receive money from Squires and to manage all kinds of business with the bank.

Miss Miller and her brother Jay Miller, manager of the Dominion Company on Bell Island, were both political supporters of Squires. It was Sir Richard's election to office that mainly contributed to his own financial problems. His bank account at the Canadian Bank of Commerce was drawn out in August, 1920. This left Miss Miller limited to the law firm's account at the Bank of Nova Scotia for office managing needs. But that account was also in trouble. Sir Richard was personally liable for an overdrawn $20,000 in notes, which was coming due. In addition, other claims were coming in and his newspaper, the *Daily Star*, was in financial trouble.

Sir Richard left these matters to Miss Miller to deal with and remained absorbed in his political work, which was requiring much travel outside the country. In August, 1920, he left Newfoundland without fixing things up with the bank. When Miss Miller attempted to enlist the bank's assistance, its manager told her he was upset that the prime minister had left the country without making arrangements with him regarding the $20,000 in notes about to come due. He refused to provide an overdraft or a loan and refused to have anything more to do with notes signed by Squires.

Squires had discussed this problem with Miller before leaving the country, however, the Hollis Walker Enquiry could not determine exactly what understanding the two had due to conflict of evidence gathered. A third person involved in the situation was Sir Richard's secretary, a Miss Saunders. Squires told Walker that before leaving he had signed and left some notes with Miss Saunders, which could be negotiated in case Miss Miller ran into problems with the banks. For whatever reason, although Miss Saunders claimed that one such note was used, Walker investigated and discovered that the notes had either disappeared or did not exist.

The Squires arrangement with his secretary was useless anyway because the Bank of Nova Scotia had advised Miss Miller that it was not prepared to accept any more notes from Sir Richard. In her efforts to bail out Squires, Miller tried other banks without success. This seems to have led her to approaching Meaney at the NLC for help.

When his business finances got to the point where operating expenses were barely being covered, Miss Miller initiated a move that expanded and eventually resulted in $100,000 to $200,000 being obtained from funds at the Board of Liquor Control. Whether she acted on her own, or had been counseled to do so, was not certain. However, Sir Richard made no attempt to place the blame on her and he accepted responsibility for amounts borrowed.

Mr. Miller made out the first cheque which was for $1,000 on November 20, 1929, and approached Meaney to cash it. It appears that he had not been asked by Squires to become involved but reluctantly did so. He cashed another $7,000 in cheques over the following weeks, under similar circumstances. Each cheque was signed, "Sir Richard A. Squires, per J. D. Miller."

When questioned during the Hollis Walker Enquiry, Meaney claimed that $3,000 of the cashed cheques was paid out of his own pocket. He did this even though his annual salary was only $2,000. To give this some perspective, in 1949, when Newfoundland joined Canada, its per capita annual income was $472.

The prime minister returned home in December, 1920, and soon after gave Miss Miller $4,000 to repay Meaney. When questioned by Walker, Meaney acknowledged the transaction and added that he repaid $3,000 to himself and put $1,000 with department funds. In March 1921, Squires rescinded Miller's signing authority but continued to borrow money from the Liquor Control, replacing the practice of issuing cheques with issuing IOUs. Between March 15th and June 20, 1921, he used twenty-four IOUs and obtained a total of $19,325.76. What did not change was Miss Miller's involvement. Now instead of signing cheques, she was signing IOUs.

Hollis Walker pointed out that all the monies from liquor sales, script or non-script, had to be deposited in the Newfoundland treasury. This was never done, and Meaney held the non-script income, which he used for personal and political purposes.

The final IOU was for $550 and was paid to Miss Miller by Meaney in July, 1922. Miller deposited it into Sir Richard's business account at the Canadian Bank of Commerce and gave Meaney a duplicate deposit slip as a receipt. In his explanation of this to Hollis Walker, Meaney said that he deposited $450 into the department account and kept $100, the amount which he claimed came from his own pocket. No evidence could be found by Walker that the deposit had been made.

In respect to the whole series of transactions with the Liquor Control, Squires was paid:

• $6,905 cheques
• $19,325.76 IOUs
• $550 deposit slips

Total = $23,630.76

Walker concluded that the total amount paid to Squires was improperly paid out of government funds and should have been repaid into the Newfoundland treasury. At the time of the enquiry, only $1,000 had been returned. He found that Miller was aware of the source of the funds, and found that all the money placed in Squires' account was for the benefit of Squires himself. He also determined that not all the monies were deposited Sir Richard's account. Some was handed to him directly, and some was used to pay outstanding bills belonging either his firm or himself.

On August 4th, while still travelling in England, Squires sent Miller a telegram which caused her even more frustration. It read, "Have telegraphed Goodland give you list Star accounts pay Murphy immediately credit arranged also 1,000 Steer note Canadian Bank renew balance." Again on August 7th, "Cable me London, Tuesday." Miller replied on August 11th, "Satisfactorily arranged."

Instead of helping to alleviate Miller's problem in handling Squires' affairs, receipt of the *Star* list only complicated matters. The *Star* list was in bad shape, and while trying to salvage some benefit from it, a stream of additional claims began piling up. It was within Miss Miller's scope to deal with such matters, and her power of attorney enabled her to negotiate loans. Unable to obtain loans from the bank, she turned to her brother, J.J. Miller, accountant for Dominion Steel, who provided her with a $40,000 loan.

After exhausting that sum, she returned to her brother requesting another loan but was flatly refused. Sir Richard had authorized Mr. Miller to use a vacant office in his building where he held personal meetings. Several of these were with Meaney. Miss Miller did not know him personally; she had met him during these visits and knew of his position with the NLC. In desperation, she visited him and negotiated a $4,000 loan which Squires later repaid. Once more, Hollis Walker ran into a brick wall when searching for documentation to support this transaction. There was none. When Walker questioned the witnesses, all provided different versions of what had happened. Sir Richard swore that he repaid the $4,000 loan and that it was the last loan he had heard of from Meaney until 1923. Miss Miller claimed the loans continued well into

1922. One thing was certain; no additional money was repaid to Meaney.

In 1921, Leslie R. Curtis became a law partner of Sir Richard. Curtis was alarmed by the state of management and office practices at the firm. He told Squires that he was not satisfied with using the office account at the Bank of Nova Scotia for anything other than purely office matters. This led to some changes in the law firm's offices. Sir Richard was upset over Miller's handling of his affairs and felt she had used the power of attorney unwisely. This resulted in the firm setting up a new trust account in the name of Leslie R. Curtis, Miller losing her power of attorney, and Mr. Fraser being appointed as accountant. Squires promised Curtis that in the future he would take a more active role in the office. This included calling at the office at 9:30 a.m. daily to deal with matters from the previous day.

Dr. Fred Rowe, an author and a colleague of Curtis during the Smallwood administration, described him:

> Curtis was acknowledged to be one of the ablest lawyers in Newfoundland. As attorney general and minister of justice he advised the government on the legal implications wherever indicated. While conservative in nature, and inclined to be suspicious and cynical regarding motives, his ability to burrow through an impasse or to ride out a crisis served Smallwood and the cabinet well on numerous occasions.[6]

The new accountant, after reviewing the firm's books, told Curtis they were "…in a deplorable condition. Records were incomplete and behind and had not been checked or balanced for years." Fraser worked hard to bring them up to date and

6 Rowe, Dr. Fred. *The Smallwood* Era. p161

consulted often with Sir Richard. He frequently had to write pages, filling in things that happened months and even years before. Despite the best efforts of Fraser, the enquiry was still faced with confusion when trying to sort out specifics. Hollis Walker stated in his report:

> These books were of very little use at the enquiry; it was always difficult and often impossible to trace a transaction through them and many important things were omitted from them altogether. Miss Miller was the person primarily responsible for them but I cannot believe that Sir Richard was entirely ignorant of their state. [7]

Sir Richard told the enquiry that Miss Miller, although planning to leave the firm to get married, continued to work at the offices at a lower salary and dealt solely with matters she was familiar with relating to insurance. Her only other duties included collecting donations for the Liberal Reform Party and keeping Squires informed on these matters. However, Miss Miller told Walker a different story. She said she was instructed by the prime minister to collect money mainly with the aid of Mr. Meaney of the NLC until July, 1922. Walker had several pieces of information that shed some light on this matter, including:

> 1. Insurance business not a firm matter but the personal concern of Sir Richard only; in the latter part of August 21st, Mr. Fraser found that the premiums collected by, or for Sir Richard had not been paid to the insurance companies for over a year and they were angrily demanding a remittance. Sir Richard asked Mr. Curtis to send a cheque on the trust account.

7 The Hollis Walker Report, 1923

2. Mr. Curtis asked Sir Richard first to put funds in that account, $5,000 was put in the account. That payment was made by Miss Miller and the deposit slip bears her name.

3. On 25 December, 1921, Miss Miller paid a sum of $3,000 into Sir Richard's account at the Canadian Bank of Commerce.

4. On 27 July, 1922, Miss Miller paid a sum of $500 into Sir Richard's account at the Canadian Bank of Commerce and left the duplicate deposit slip in the hands of Mr. Meaney.

5. As late as August, 1922, the manager of the Bank of Commerce was dealing with Miss Miller with reference to deposits which should have been made to Richard's letter of credit account.

Rumours were spreading around the NLC that Meaney was overstocking on liquor supplies. Still, the board paid no attention to Meaney. Things changed during the Hollis Walker Enquiry. Those targeted by the investigation acted strangely and were evasive during questioning. During June, 1923, the offices of the NLC were broken into and records stolen. The constabulary was called in to investigate. Meaney was obviously upset by the incident and, according to investigating officers, he said, "It's the work of the prime minister." When questioned by Walker, he denied making the statement. Meanwhile, he sensed his relationship with Squires changing.

Because of the burglary, Meaney was suspended from his position, and heard a rumour that criminal charges were to be laid against him. He became very bitter towards Squires, and sought out legal advice. Acting on this advice, he gave his full story to the Justice Department. A justice official called Walker's attention to the conduct of the prime minister, bearing upon his credibility at the enquiry. Walker already found Sir Richard's conduct strange. He explained:

> Though he discussed the charge with Ministers and members of his party, he never attempted to offer any explanation of it, and he did not deny it. Though the Minister of Justice waited on him with reference to the charge, he told him that he himself had seen the cheques and IOUs and used words which he [Sir Richard] took to be an invitation to explain and no explanation or denial was forthcoming. Yet, according to his own evidence, he realized in December 1922 from the term of reference then published, that he was implicated in this section of the enquiry. He did not ask for inspection of the documents or for any particulars with regard to them, nor, did he give any instructions to his counsel on the matter and on the first day of the hearing his counsel, Mr. Howley, K.C. stated to me, and I have no doubt truthfully: 'I would like to point out that I have now for the first time intimation that my client is interested in any way in this particular head [heading] of the Commission.'[8]

Walker firmly believed that Sir Richard had long known that he was implicated in the scandal and the allegations against him.

Curtis interviewed both Miss Miller and Mr. Meaney regarding statements they provided to justice officials for use at the enquiry in an attempt to adjust the financial side of the liquor control question, with the expectation that Walker might be willing to withdraw that issue. Walker was not impressed, and concluded that Sir Richard's part in connection with

8 Hollis Walker Commission,1923

Mr. Miller's statement did not raise his opinion of the prime minister's straightforwardness.

It became apparent during the enquiry that Mr. Miller was willing to do anything he could to avoid the ordeal of the witness box. However, Meaney was viewed as trying to shield the prime minister with the hope of regaining his position at the NLC. This was indicated in his statement to Curtis that he was not trying to avoid "…taking his own medicine." Miss Miller and Meaney opened the door for Squires' lawyer to criticize and go on the offensive. Walker was reluctant to give credibility to the testimony of the two, because of their admission of wrongdoing, without corroborating evidence from documents and other circumstances.

Mr. Meaney was on friendly terms with Sir Richard during the loan transactions, but as time passed and he was not given the position of permanent controller of the NLC, his attitude changed. In respect to this, Walker said:

> This was an additional reason for scrutinizing his word, though I do not accept the contention that his evidence, which was given with engaging if shameless candor, is to be wholly disregarded. Both he and Miss Miller regarded the payments as of a temporary character. They expected that Sir Richard would redeem them, that the money would be returned to the Department, and no great harm would be done. Moreover, very little of Mr. Meaney's evidence directly touched Sir Richard in this part of the enquiry and the question of Sir Richard's complicity depended much more upon the evidence of Miss Miller. It was suggested that she had also become Sir Richard's enemy, and had entered into a conspiracy with Mr. Meaney. I could see no sign whatever of this.[9]

9 Ibid

After hearing all testimony, Walker concluded that despite some lapses of memory and a few inaccuracies in her testimony that Miss Miller was indeed telling the truth to the best of her ability. In assessing Sir Richard's evidence, Walker noted that although as a public man and prime minister he was always open to attack and misrepresentation of his position, accomplishments were always kept in mind as well as his credibility as a witness.

In respect to Sir Richard's complicity in the NLC and other loan transactions, Walker found:

1. That before he left St. John's for Europe in August, 1920, Sir Richard Squires included Mr. Meaney among those whom he specifically authorized Miss Miller to apply to for financial help.

2. That when Meaney was repaid $4,000, it was on account of a larger sum due, and that Sir Richard Squires did not in any way indicate to Miss Miller displeasure that she had been to Mr. Meaney or desire that she not go to him again.

3. That Miss Miller kept Sir Richard informed of all the various amounts that she obtained from Mr. Meaney, and from time to time conveyed to him requests from Mr. Meaney that the amounts should be repaid. It may well be that Sir Richard did not at any particular moment know the exact total of his indebtedness. Mr. Meaney was too suspicious and too wary to bring into existence a written list, but he knew the approximated figure and he knew how substantial it was.[10]

10 The Hollis Walker Enquiry, 1923

Miss Miller never claimed she told Sir Richard that her source of loans was coming from the NLC, but she said that situation was always understood and there was no need to tell him. Walker accepted that as fact. He said:

It was obvious Sir Richard knew all about Mr. Meaney, his aggressive politics, his fluent pen and his slender purse. Mr. Meaney had followed many callings. Immediately before he went to the Liquor Control he held a post on the staff of the Daily Star at $35 weekly and his income was supplemented by other journalistic work. Occasionally he was involved in lumber ventures. He was a poor man, as Sir Richard intimated, he had to be fed and clothed by someone. He gave up the Star and went to the NLC for $50 weekly while retaining his other income from writing. He was still a poor man quite unable to provide any large sum from his own resources.[11]

Walker also found that until 1923, Sir Richard was not aware that Meaney had been feathering his nest by accepting hidden commissions from suppliers and that any amount of personal savings, like $20,000 in two years, was entirely beyond his visible resources. In fact, Sir Richard told Hollis Walker, "No one could take large sums from Mr. Meaney at that time without the strongest suspicion that public money was being used and that he would regard four thousand dollars as a large amount." Yet, in December, 1921, no less than $9,000 was obtained from Meaney for Sir Richard. Walker concluded:

That Sir Richard Squires realized in August, 1920, that money might be obtained for him through Mr.

11 Ibid

Meaney from the funds of the Liquor Department, and that after his return he realized that it had been so obtained, and was, being so obtained; that he accepted the use and benefit of over twenty thousand dollars, so obtained with knowledge of their tainted history, and he made himself a receiver and accomplice in Mr. Meaney's wrong.[12]

It is ironic that Sir Richard Squires, who had campaigned successfully in the 1919 election to reform government and rid Newfoundlander of 'her grafters,' found himself knee deep in scandals. The bootlegging income was only the top of the iceberg. As Hollis Walker probed deeper, he found other areas of corruption.

The Hollis Walker Enquiry found:

A loophole in the Prohibition legislation, permitting the Controller of the Newfoundland Liquor Board to approve exceptions to that rule, opened the door for political corruption. The Liquor Control Department was little more than a legal 'front' for a large-scale bootlegging operation directed by the acting controller, J.T. Meaney, ex-journalist of the *Daily Star* and appointee of Sir Richard Squires.[13]

Historian Assessed Walker Report

Describing The Hollis Walker Report, published on March 21, 1924, S.J.R. Noel observed:

It remains a classic document of the times, setting out in some twenty-five thousand words a damning indictment not only of the persons involved but of

12 Ibid
13 This and more information on political corruption in Newfoundland prior to 1949 can be found in *Newfoundland's Era of Corruption* (Creative Publishers.)

the political system under which they were able to flourish.

Regarding the repeal of Prohibition in 1924, Noel observed:

> The abuses arising from the 'noble experiment' had helped bring the law, politics, and even, because of their indiscriminate sale of 'prescriptions,' the medical profession into disrepute; after the Hollis Walker enquiry, in particular, with its revelations of how far the corruption had spread, there arose an overwhelming consensus in favour of repeal. [14]

14 Noel, S.J.R. *Politics in Newfoundland.* p180

Chapter 8

Coast Guard vs. Rum-runners

A uthorities were fighting a losing battle during Prohibition in the United States. On the country's Atlantic coast, the contact boats used by mobsters to receive contraband entering Rum Row from St. Pierre and St. John's, Newfoundland, were the major problem faced by the American Coast Guard. To combat this problem, the Americans sought Britain's help to enlist the cooperation of Newfoundland and France to help to control St. Pierre. France flatly refused to cooperate and Newfoundland ignored Britain's efforts. The Americans were hoping that both places would introduce Prohibition.

In the beginning, the syndicate rum-running vessels outclassed the Coast Guard vessels in speed and, for a while, held the upper hand in the battle. The majority of rum-runners were able to out manoeuvre the destroyers used by Coast Guard. According to Prohibition historian Malcolm Willoughby:

> Many contact boats which were owned by the syndicates were constructed in yards where Coast Guard contracts also had been let. The [crime] bosses discovered the exact speeds of the new craft being built for their adversaries, and they changed their speed plans accordingly.[1]

---

1 Willoughby, Malcolm. *Rum War at Sea.* U.S. Government Printing Office, Washington. pp61. 1964.

To combat the advantage the mobsters held in this battle, the Coast Guard developed a series of strategies. Willoughby explained:

> It became more and more a battle of wits, in which the rum-runners also used tricks and tactic to throw the Coast Guard of balance, to evade capture in chase, to hide or destroy evidence, and to produce misleading intelligence. The Coast Guard was not at all backward in productive countermoves.[2]

Rum-runners Tactics

In the following case, the rum-runners managed to escape arrest and save most of their contraband liquor. The Coast Guard watched from a distance as cases of liquor were lowered from the rum ship, *Thorndyke*, onto a mob contact boat. Instead of full speed ahead to intercept the transaction, the cutter lowered her launch hoping to intercept the unloading without alarming those involved. However, the three men in the contact boat saw the lowering of the launch and quickly climbed back aboard the rum-runner. When the launch arrived, they found twenty cases of liquor on the motorboat, but when they attempted to board the *Thorndyke* they met resistance from the crew, which outnumbered them. The customs officers retreated while the rum-runner and crew escaped.

The Decoy Tactic

One clever deception was to have a bunch of small contact boats go out to meet the offshore rum vessels together. The slowest among them would be used to take aboard a few cases of liquor, while the rest handled full loads. The slow boat

2 Ibid

acted as a decoy in cases when the transaction was detected by a cutter. Once the decoy got the cutter's attention, it would move to escape causing the cutter to give chase.

While the chase was taking place, the others would speed away in the other direction and were usually successful in landing its cargo, where gangsters awaited to take possession and deliver it to the bosses.

Get Rid of the Evidence

Radio distress signals were often used by rum-runners to mislead the cutters. Such was the case when a distress signal was sent out that a ship was in trouble off the North Carolina coast. The vessel did not have a radio aboard. However, the aim of the rum-runners was to distract the cutters and draw them away from their drop-off point. It worked so well that multiple contact boats succeeded in landing their loads to their destined delivery points along Rum Row.

Willoughby pointed out:

> When the cutters went to sea to picket and scout the vessels of Rum Row, many of the latter shifted position constantly, thus adding difficulties for the Coast Guard vessels watching them. Despite the rum-runners' intelligence activities which had become well developed, this complicated the problem for contact boats in locating their source supply.[3]

Rum-runners used a technique, though not always successful, to get rid of as much evidence as possible when capture seemed imminent. The American cutter, *Gresham*, was circling a fleet of about thirty rum-running vessels, when one of the rum-runners was seen alongside a mother ship to

3 Ibid

107

load its share of contraband for smuggling into the United States. The captain of the cutter shouted, "Full steam ahead!" going all out towards the smugglers. The tug, *Albatross*, just as quickly, raced from the scene and led the *Gresham* on a fifty-mile, zig-zag chase, lasting over four hours.

From a distance behind, the captain of the cutter witnessed the smugglers tossing kegs of liquor overboard to get rid of the needed evidence before being caught. The chase came to an end when the cutter fired several shots over the bow of the rum-runner. The smugglers felt confident because they had gotten rid of their entire load of rum, leaving no grounds for an arrest.

They got quite a surprise, when their vessel was boarded by members of the Coast Guard, who took possession of the boat, arrested the entire crew and threw its captain in the cutter's brig because of his disruptive attitude during the arrest. When the captain protested, "We're not carrying any liquor; you have no grounds to make an arrest!" He was informed that during the chase, the cutter had recovered several kegs of liquor.

During Prohibition in St. John's, a rum-running vessel manned by a crew of Newfoundlanders was delivering a load of contraband from St. Pierre to connections in St. John's. They eyed the customs control vessel leaving the wharf, near Prescott Street. The waters entering the harbour that day were rough and the smugglers were being rocked back and forth.

As customs slowly passed them, they would wave to its crew while the side of the boat facing the cutter was on the high end of the rocking waves but, while this distracted the customs officers, smugglers on the low side of the rocking boat tossed kegs of rum into the harbour. They successfully passed the cutter, which sailed out of the harbour and headed towards the south coast.

Meanwhile, the rum-runners tied up at the wharf and its crew lowered a couple of lifeboats. With the customs boat out of sight, they rowed out to the mouth of the harbour to recover their cargo, but they had a shocking surprise waiting for them.

While they were conning the customs boat, Battery fishermen were keeping a close eye on what was being tossed over the side, and figuring out what was actually happening. The Battery fishermen wasted no time, and before the smugglers were able to return, they had recovered it, hidden it, and continued on with their regular daily chores. Prohibition smugglers referred to those who hijacked their cargoes in those days as pirates.

Beachcombers Pirates

Rum-runners landing a supply for contacts in St. John's sometimes hid the contraband in a deserted cove. Such a case happened several times near Petty Harbour. On one occasion, a small fishing schooner from Conception Bay, after leaving Petty Harbour, set into one such cove and while looking around found a large supply of kegs and cases of liquor. He had heard of this smugglers practice and boasted to the others, "It's our lucky day."

The crew loaded the schooner and carried it to their home port in Conception Bay, where they found a suitable hiding place for it. They knew the real owners would have their men out trying to track it down. Not too long after, some men from St. John's appeared in the community asking questions about anyone who had come into a large amount of liquor. Their secret was kept! It was later learned that the shipment was destined for a well-known St. John's merchant.

There were many cases of beachcombers finding hidden caches of contraband liquor. To deal with this problem, the bigger rum-runners found a means of discarding and recovering their illegal supplies. Strong manila lines were attached to connect the cases of liquor and were connected to partially submerged buoys. Generally, this practice went well.

An alternate scheme was to use rafts to carry deliveries to shorelines along Rum Row, where the American gangsters waited for delivery. The main problem encountered by this method was the changing tides, which hindered the course of the raft.

Destroyer Cutters at Disadvantage

When destroyers were used to combat rum-running, their inability to make quick, sharp turns proved to be a disadvantage. When these craft were in pursuit of rum-running vessels, the rum-runner would quickly make a U-turn and speed towards the destroyer, pass it and often escaped arrest. However, this was usually successful in cases where the rum-runners were able to emit a smokescreen to mislead their pursuer before turning.

Destroyers practiced circling the rum-runner and then hauling to. This proved a problem on the Newfoundland Grand Banks when fog swept in and the rum-runner, many with experienced Newfoundland or Maritime sea skippers, made an escape. Radar had not yet been invented and, therefore, it was not an option during this period.

Lieutenant Commander J.E. Whitbeck in command of the destroyer, *Ericsson*, found an effective way of getting around the International Rules of the Sea, which prohibited using a searchlight beam onto the bridge of another ship. He recognized a vessel in the area as a rum-runner and called its skipper telling him, "Look, captain, we're going to test some machine guns tonight so please keep your lights on so we won't accidentally hit you." The destroyer was required to test its machine guns monthly. The smuggler agreed and left his lights on.

Aboard the *Ericsson*, the crew were busy loading the guns and placing them in position. The rum-runner became suspicious, doused the lights and gave the command, "Full speed ahead!" He was too late.

The machine guns opened fire, although not directly at the rum-runner, it was enough for its skipper to surrender. The crew and ship were taken under arrest.

Rum-runners often used the technique of grounding to stop cutters; they led the large cutters who were chasing them into shoal water, grounding them. The rum-runner *Albatross* was a tug that brought many cargoes of liquor to Rum Row by transferring its cargo onto a waiting contact boat and towing it to its rendezvous. Usually, the Coast Guard did not suspect tugs with tows. The gangsters on shore arranged for special type of ships to be used for this purpose. A popular source for them was the garbage scows owned and operated by the city of New York.

To service the multi-billion dollar bootlegging industry in the United States, rum-runners were often inventive. In response to better cutters, they developed a low-hulled speed boat with flat bottom and a sharp chine line with a pillbox-type pilot house.

Military historian Willoughby described these as:

These vessels were powered with a Liberty type marine conversion of the famous aircraft engine of World War I, and had two, three, or four engines. The craft were often armoured. Some had pilot house armour concealed by outside paneling; others had armour plate openly bolted on the outside of the hull to protect gasoline tanks and engines. On their run in with a load, islands were made on deck by building bulwarks of liquor several cases thick to protect the crew who could not get behind the armour of the pilot house or engine room.[4]

These craft could carry cargoes of up to 1,600 cases.

4 Willoughby, Malcolm. *Rum War at Sea*.1964.pp65

The Newfoundland rum-running fleet's primary task was getting the liquor cargoes to the contact boats along Rum Row. When that task ended these crews could breathe a sigh of relief and head home until the next delivery. However, those accepting delivery had their own problems getting the contraband to the string of destinations along the coast.

The use of World War I destroyers was certainly effective in reducing the flow of liquor into the United States. The risk for all involved in rum-running, bootlegging and the underground gambling casinos was increasing. The rum-runners in the Atlantic City area of Rum Row came up with an unexpected strategy to improve their lot. If the Coast Guard was going to confiscate their caches of liquor, thereby reducing their income, they would respond in a way that would replace the income being lost. The answer was simple — "Strike!" And strike they did!"

The one dollar a case being paid at the time doubled to two dollars. A crime reporter for *The New York Times* quoted one rum-runner as commenting:

> We go out and we get the stuff and start back. We're fired on, and if we're close pressed very often the cases go overboard. If we come back empty-handed, we get no pay at all. Absolutely nuttin'. What we want is fairness.[5]

Newfoundland Rum-runners Challenged by Destroyer Force

Rum-runners out of St. John's, Port aux Basques and St. Pierre were well-aware of the U.S. Coast Guard's surveillance along Rum Row, but had no idea how well they were organized. The Coast Guard operated using the traditional naval organization plan. This plan utilized three divisions of six: one division was based in Boston, a second one was

5 Ibid

centered at the Destroyer Force Headquarters in New London, and the third was at Statin Island, New York.

Willoughby outlined how these operated:

> At the beginning of the dark of the moon or after off-shore boats had been dispersed by a gale, a sweep by a division of destroyers was made at high speed from the Virginia Capes to the Canadian Border, [Rum Row] following the coastline, the destroyers at double visibility distance apart. This usually meant an area of 100 to 120 miles offshore was searched. In patrolling under normal conditions, each destroyer of a division was assigned a definite area. Each day in the early morning a search was made of the area to locate rum-runners, using either a standard Navy search plan or a specialized Coast Guard method. At night, an offshore rum-runner was picketed by each destroyer; other rummies farther inshore were assigned to the six-bitters [smaller speed craft].

Customs officials and Coast Guard personnel had to remain continuously alert for the new tricks and schemes developed by the rum-runners to avoid detection. Among the practices detected included: false bottoms in boats, secret compartments, false partitions, double holds and hiding cases of liquor among cargoes of fish.

Chapter 9

Prohibition Threatened
North America's Oldest Regatta

When the rum and ginger beer,
Your poor sinking heart to cheer,
sure you'd never lose your head
but take things coolly.
And the whiskey is so mild
you may give it to a child
they'd call it lemonade in Bally Haly.

Johnny Burke's Regatta program, 1898

The most historic Regatta in North America, the Royal St. John's Regatta, survived its beginnings in the 1820s despite disease, a poor economy and two world wars. Yet, the most consistent and challenging factor to its survival was none of the above. From its beginnings in the early 1820s, liquor and rowdiness sparked strong opposition to the "Day of the Races" and in many years, forced its cancellation. Throughout the entire nineteenth century, the presence of liquor at lakeside on Regatta Day remained a serious threat to its existence.

Little wonder, considering the prevalence of alcohol consumption during the early years. During the 1820s, when the Quidi Vidi Regatta started, Newfoundland had a population of 20,000 with 6,000 living in St. John's. Liquor was a major part of life as evidenced by the fact that in just one year during the 1820s, 220,000 gallons of rum was consumed by the Newfoundland population. This did not include brandy, gin, wine and beer, which were also available.

The Bunch of Grapes, owned by a Mr. Best, was a tavern favourably located for early Regattas at Bulley's Farm, on the north side of Quidi Vidi Lake. In addition to the Bunch of Grapes tavern, liquor patrons often brought their own brews to lakeside on Regatta Day. Because of this, it was very difficult to control abuse of liquor during the first years of Regatta.

Ladies Boycott the Races

The first Regattas held in the 1820s were enthusiastically anticipated by the men of the city. However, the ladies were not as pleased with the new social and sporting event. In 1828, the women of St. John's attracted some public attention by boycotting the Regatta.

The Newfoundlander offered an explanation of the boycott following the Regatta. It reported:

> We feel assured it was just a retaliation upon their parts for the inattention with which they have been treated for the last three or four years; and certainly, they could not adopt a more effectual mode of punishment than by absenting themselves from every scene of amusement and proving to the beaus how joyless and dim such pleasure, when not enlivened by their smiles, but that, Whether sunn'd in the tropics, or chill'd at the pole; if woman be there, there is happiness, too. We would strongly recommend the Ladies until a proper return be made for all their kindness to persevere in this line of conduct–and they will soon be able to dictate their own terms.

And what distracted the men from the women at the 1826 and 1827 Regattas? Early records show heavy betting heightened interest in the boat races and there was excessive consumption of, "the national" (rum). Little wonder the ladies felt ignored.

Dampened Spirits

The consumption of liquor at the races often dampened the enthusiasm of many. The Regatta, which was started to relieve summer boredom, became a widely anticipated festive season. Men would go on drinking binges that often lasted for a week, or more, after Regatta Day. This inspired strong opposition from several groups. First, many businessmen opposed the Regatta because labourers failed to return to work and delays were experienced in unloading cargo ships. Housewives joined in the opposition because when their husbands went on binges, families were left without money and food until the men sobered enough to return to work. The third source of opposition came from temperance groups who organized all opponents of the Regatta.

Following the 1845 Regatta, opposition was strong enough to put an end to the Regatta. At least it seemed that way. But those who favoured the summer Regatta battled to restore it. Their efforts paid off, and in 1851 the Regatta was revived. The races continued until 1860, but were again cancelled for reasons that included fear of liquor abuse and violence. From 1860 to 1870 there were no Regattas held at Quidi Vidi. However, boat races were held on St. John's Harbour in 1865. The political and economic uncertainty of the 1860s, and the violence associated with it, caused authorities to become concerned over continuing the Regatta. It was felt that a public gathering of this magnitude combined with the liquor abuse and rowdiness that went with it could spark violence.

More Problems

Once again, public interest in reviving the Regatta succeeded and the races resumed with enthusiasm in 1871. By 1875, opposition was again mounting against the Regatta. An article in *The Newfoundlander* in August, 1875, referred to drunkenness and rowdiness at lakeside and stated, "... viewed in this light is felt that, however desirable an occasional break in our work-a-day monotony, it is made to cost too dearly and hard though it seems, had better be avoided than purchased at the price of such consequences." In 1877, the same newspaper called upon authorities to increase the number of police officers at the Regatta and to restrict the number of liquor licences.

Drunkenness and rowdiness were not just spectator vices. At the 1881 Regatta, a drunken committee member insulted a senior citizen inside the committee tent. Some rowers publicly demanded that in the future sobriety and courtesy be requirements in selecting committee members. Sometimes, little respect was shown towards on-duty police officers on Regatta Day. One newspaper reported in August, 1885, that an ordinarily well-mannered longshoremen, "...had the audacity to place Constable Pynn in a horizontal position." When Pynn recovered the drunk was taken to the lock-up.

This was followed by several letters in newspapers calling for an end to the Regatta. The problem of gambling at lakeside often went hand-in-hand with the abuse of liquor. One letter read, "It's outrageous to see clerks betting $10 and merchants $100 on a single race."

The Governor Loved It!

The most prominent advocate for the Regatta in 1886 was Governor Des Voeux. He responded to suggestions that the Regatta be cancelled with his statement, "I regret very much to hear that there are those that regard this meeting with disfavour. I cannot but think they are completely wrong in their sense of proportion. Some are bound to misbehave in any such gathering..."

Sometimes acts of liquor-inspired bravado placed lives at risk. Such was the case in 1890, when a drunken spectator jumped into the lake and tried to race the *Myrtle* up the pond. When he got in trouble and began drowning, Constable Jim Fitzgerald dove into the water in full uniform. With hundreds of spectators watching, the police officer grabbed the drowning man with one arm and with the other grabbed onto a boat passing by. The boat landed the duo safely ashore, amid loud cheering and applause from the crowds.

Poor Congdon's Spruce Beer!

Spruce beer contained alcohol in the 1890s, and in 1894, Johnny Congdon of Lazy Bank (Pleasant Street) had grand plans to make money selling it at the races. He had carefully brewed four large tubs of spruce beer to sell at lakeside on Derby Day, as the Regatta was sometimes called. However, on the day before the races poor Congdon suffered a misfortune. While he was at lakeside constructing his concession tent, his home on Lazy Bank caught fire.

Unable to curtail the flames, his wife bravely decided to sacrifice the beer to save the house. Aided by neighbours, she began dumping the four beer tubs over the fire. Needless to say, Congdon wasn't a happy man when he returned home to find his home partly destroyed and his beer supply evaporated. He took a great deal of ribbing from neighbours and friends. Too add insult to injury, his neighbour at lakeside sold spruce beer and erected a sign over the tent which read: "Spruce Beer...good for drinking too!"

Fogarty-Flowers Brawl

The 1844 Regatta stands out in history, not because of any record-breaking races, but because it was at that event where William Fogarty was killed. Among the crowd on the banks of Quidi Vidi that day were Jane Flowers, her husband,[1] Billy Fogarty and Paddy Cowman. All four had been tipping the bottle and an argument erupted between Fogarty and Mr. Flowers.

Fogarty delivered a powerful right fist to Flowers' head, causing him to drop to the ground. As the crowd's attention was diverted from the races on the pond, to the Fogarty-Flowers brawl, Jane came to her husband's defence by throwing a rock at Fogarty. Cowman's fist connected with Fogarty's head around the same time.

Fogarty fell to the ground but did not die immediately. He lingered on for two hours and then passed away. Jane Flowers and Patrick Cowman were arrested and tried in Supreme Court on the charge of manslaughter. At the trial, the two doctors who had attended to Fogarty on the day he was killed testified for the defence.

Their evidence surprised the people of St. John's. It showed that neither the punches nor the rock had caused Fogarty's death. According to their evidence, the excitement of the fight had caused blood vessels in his brain to burst. Medical evidence showed that death could not have been caused by the blows because the body was sound and uninjured.

The jury took only twenty minutes to arrive at a verdict, not guilty. It was a Regatta to remember.

The Regatta of 1891 also had a tragic ending. A twenty-year-old man named Fleming drank too much liquor, fell asleep near the lake and suffocated. Friends discovered him as people left the area at the conclusion of the Regatta.

---

1 Husband's name not mentioned in records.

Pooh-Bah's of The Regatta!

In 1904, the licensing board which controlled the sale of liquor refused all requests to sell spirits at the Regatta. Some patrons were so angered by the decision that they sent letters to the newspapers. One person's letter in *The Evening Telegram* stated, "If the board made its decision known two weeks ago, there'd be no Regatta in 1904. There are too many Pooh-Bahs in this country." sgd. Buttercup. (*Buttercup* was a race boat in the nineteenth century). A second letter said, "Are the people of this country not to be trusted on a race course where liquor is in close proximity without becoming fit subjects for strait jackets." The law did not prevent some from bringing their own to the races. One such person jumped into the lake and vowed that he could race the *Blue Peter* up the pond. He was pulled out by the police.

A verse from Johnny Burke's 1898 Regatta program speaks of liquor at the old-time Regattas. He wrote:

And meself was no way shy
for to wet the other eye
and then with rolling gait for home I faces.
And it's many and many a load
I slept off on the road
Oh, the morning of the Terra Nova Races.

Shebeen Tents

During the Prohibition era police were always on, "...the Qui Vie for shebeen tents." These were bootlegger tents which conducted thriving business at lakeside. To avoid detection, they used passwords in order for patrons to gain access. Some operators made themselves known only to a selected crowd. The committee had a liquor-related rule regarding spares during the 1920s and 1930s. All spares had to remain sober, at least until the boats passed the committee tent.

With the large numbers of troops coming and going in St. John's during the 1940s, it is remarkable how well the liquor problem was controlled. After the 1942 Regatta, a city magistrate commented on the absence, "...of the usual run of drunks." Inspector Case said that not a single arrest had been made at Quidi Vidi. Yet, the era was not without incident.

In 1945, an American sailor inebriated on homebrew rolled up his sleeves and challenged one and all to fisticuffs. He was doing well until he came up against a fellow named Bradbury from Torbay, "...a giant of a man who quickly disposed of his adversary."

Committee Scandal

During the 1950s, a scandal developed relating to the Regatta committee's fundraising efforts. The scandal was uncovered after cheques, made payable to the committee, were found blowing around lakeside. Some of the funds collected were finding its way into the pockets of two of the fundraisers, who spent much of the cash getting drunk. The committee saw the need to review, and tightened up its fundraising programs. It was John Perlin, a former president of the Regatta committee and Regatta Hall of Fame member, who devised the system of issuing receipts and land use permits.

Although the problem of theft was effectively dealt with, the tradition of committee members bringing liquor into the Higgins Marquee and the boathouse continued until 1978. Queen Elizabeth and the Duke of Edinburgh visited the Regatta that year. John Perlin successfully appealed to committee members to discontinue the old custom in order to present a show of competence to the Royal visitors. Recalling that eventful year, Perlin later commented, "...it was not hard to sell and seemed to be an idea that won instant acceptance."

Since 1978, liquor has not been consumed by members on Regatta Day.

Battling the Drunks

Mike Murphy, author of *Pathways to Yesteryear*, was a member of the local constabulary during the 1930s and often worked a shift at lakeside on Regatta Day. Reminiscing in the late 1960s about the old-time Regattas, Murphy recalled that, "There were times when the annual Regatta at Quidi Vidi Pond was more like a battlefield than anything else. We'd charge in with our night sticks and those drunks would fight right back."

Murphy recalled that police made few arrests in those days. Instead, they would take the drunks to a tent where they would sleep it off. On Regatta Day, the whole force would be on duty. "Today there will be about forty-five constabulary members on duty at lakeside. Their job will be mainly traffic and crowd control, as few drunks have been seen at the annual event in recent years."

Murphy noted that in earlier times:

They had the hop beer tents and people could get drunk at the Regatta. The hop beer, occasionally flavoured with Beaver tobacco plugs, was pretty potent stuff and the men who drank it were a pretty aggressive bunch...belligerent and tough, not like the alcoholics you have today who can barely lift a hand toward you, these men were mean.

He continued:

When they got out of hand we went at them without clubs. We rarely arrested them but brought them into a tent to sleep it off. They had to be really bad before they were arrested.

Murphy said that sometimes you could tell a fight was "...in the making." He gave as an example, the story of the hop beer tent at the head of the pond. He said:

There was one guy who had a hop beer tent right at the head of the pond and every now and then you'd see him run out of the tent, scoop up a bucket of water from the lake and throw it in the beer keg when he got a bit low. This was usually where the trouble broke out.

Murphy concluded:

Also common were the lost kids. There'd be about 10 at a time in the police tent all squawking and we'd have to wait for their parents to come for them... eventually we'd buy them candy and stuff until they were calmed.

In those days children sang the following verse which summed up some of the old-time Regattas:

Coming home from the races,
Bleeding noses and cut faces,
and we're all as drunk as blazes
Coming home from the Races[2]

2 Fitzgerald, Jack. *A Day at the Races.* Creative Publishers. 2003.

Chapter 10

100 Years of Prohibition Humour and Song

During the era of Prohibition, many amusing anecdotes survived, along with songs inspired by the times. This chapter is a pourpori of historic gems.

An amusing anecdote was often told about one St. John's doctor who sympathized with poor drinkers who couldn't afford to pay the one-dollar script fee charged. He wrote out so many scripts that it got to the point where even the controller employees could not read them.

One day a gentleman of the town mistakenly handed the clerk a receipt for a payment given to the doctor which was signed by the doctor. The clerk quickly read it and passed him a bottle of Scotch! The script given to him by the doctor was still in his pocket when he got home.[2]

During the script era, a popular piece of humour going around town went like this:

When Doc Smith finished issuing a script to a patient he commented, "Of course you're sick, and now name four of your friends who are sick and that will be five dollars."

This system of issuing prescriptions for liquor to a patient allowed individual patients to obtain separate scripts for family members or friends by just telling the doctor their names and paying the dollar fee for each.

One doctor being tried told the judge that he had every right under the Prohibition law to issue eight ounces of liquor a day to a person needing it for medical purposes. The judge, looking over his docket for the day, spoke loudly enough for

2 "The Big Drought" – (Sic) Phillips, *Newfoundland Lifestyles*

all to hear, "I don't have a problem with them, but we have a few coming up today who went away carrying puncheons." The prosecutor injected, "Perhaps they had headaches." The judge shot back, "Well, if they didn't before, they certainly did later."

Surprisingly this is a true anecdote. The doctor in question had a sharp lawyer representing him. Holding an open copy of the Prohibition law in his hand, he effectively explained to the court:

> The fact of this case is that the medical doctor is the only person allowed to make judgement on who gets a prescription and he has the right to issue one eight ounce drink per day 'or larger quantities if necessary.' Only the doctor has that authority. A puncheon of rum for medicinal reasons is legally permitted.

He won his case.

A fellow named Paddy Fowler from the Southern Shore used to visit St. John's every Saturday with a wagon full of vegetables, which he sold door to door in the city. He'd always stop at an east end shebeen for refreshments before starting on the long journey home. On one such visit, Paddy came out of the shebeen to find that his horse and wagon had disappeared. He returned to the place and told Casey to pour him another beer. Then he pounded his fist on the bar and roared, "Me harse and wagon is not where I left it. By the lard Jasus and all that's holy, if it's not back where I left it by the time I finish this beer, the same thing that happened last week up at Bay Bulls is going to happen here, and ya won't want that to happen!" He struck the bar with his fist again for emphasis.

His warning was received with utter silence and then a shuffling of feet as some men, sensing trouble, left the bar. Paddy finished his beer and as he turned to leave, he said in a loud voice, "Be-Jasus, the harse better be there!" It was!

His angry warning had worked. A fellow from Mundy Pond asked Paddy, "Tell me, sir, what happened at Bay Bulls last week?"

"Be-Jasus, me harse wasn't there and I had to walk home," replied Paddy.

During the 1930s, Paddy Fowler of Cappahayden was upset when someone began stealing his hens. Paddy decided to set a trap to catch the thieves. The next night, he and his brother-in-law, Tom Cahill, hid in the shed which was used as a hen house. Armed with a bottle of Screech, they made themselves comfortable while waiting for the hen thieves to show up. After a short time, they felt the shed sway a little. Tom told Paddy, "No need to worry it's just the wind," and the two continued to enjoy their drink.

After two hours, Tom Cahill, fed up waiting, announced that he was going home, saying, "Let's call it a night, Paddy, they'll not be here tonight."

Tom stepped out of the shed and found himself on a motor truck, which was moving slowly along the road. The hen thieves had struck again and were stealing the hen house with all that was in it — including Tom and Paddy!

The following anecdote has survived from the era of scripts and wood alcohol. After two men were hospitalized after drinking wood alcohol, and one of them had died, the other was on trial for supplying the substance. At trial, the following exchange took place between the doctor and prosecutor.

"Doctor when did you perform the autopsy on the victim?" queried the prosecutor.

"At 10:15 a.m., Tuesday June 6th," replied the doctor.

"And he was dead at the time?" Asked the prosecutor.

"No. He was just lying there and wondering why I was performing an autopsy," answered the doctor.

Another piece of Prohibition humour involves the notorious, but small, rum-running vessel the *Nellie J. Banks* during one of her Prohibition lives as a Newfoundland-registered vessel sailing under the Newfoundland flag. Her Newfoundland crew in this escapade included Newfoundland-born Captain Edward Seeley, Master Joseph Vatcher of Burgeo, George Mackay of Nova Scotia, Eli Pardy from Harbour Mille, and an unnamed Newfoundland cook.

Newfoundland was no longer under Prohibition, the United States had it, as did some Canadian provinces. During 1926, this little rum-runner was involved in what the mob considered a large scale operation, with a mission to land illegal Demerara rum at a port in Prince Edward Island. Two American gangsters were financing the trip and arranged to accept the delivery. That is providing they got passed customs and the R.C.M.P. First, they had to get the cargo to the eastern point of Prince Edward Island, where it would be reshipped to St. Pierre.

When the two mob guys asked Captain Seeley to see the charts, the captain told them not to worry because he knew the waters in the area to the French islands like the back of his hand. Master Mackay was less convinced, and when he asked Captain Seeley if he could have a look at the charts, the captain told him, "The dog ate 'em." Don't you worry now son, all the rocks are underneath the water?" Captain Seeley turned out to be as good as he boasted and the run ended in success which pleased the hoods.

Desperate for Rum

In 1918, a man trying to raise money for "a drink of the national" stole his wife's boots and tried to sell them. He was caught by a police officer on patrol and the next day the incident was reported in *The Evening Telegram* as follows:

Saturday afternoon Sergeant Mackey discovered an outport man buying a pair of woman's boots from a resident of the city. Knowing that the man was a hard drinker, he discovered that he was selling the boots for a couple of shillings to buy drink. Sergeant Mackey took the boots and restored them to the unfortunate wife and sent the seller and would-be purchaser about their business.

Regatta Day Humor

A humorous incident took place during a Regatta held during Prohibition at Quidi Vidi Lake. It has survived as a popular anecdote for almost 100 years. I first heard it told by Jimmy Higgins, politician, Supreme Court judge and a president of the Royal St. John's Regatta Committee. During the 1920s, it was traditional for a few committee members to be assigned the task of firing the gun to start each race. Each member would usually take every third or fourth race, so that everyone could have some time to enjoy the day. On one occasion at about 5:00 p.m., one of the starters had been having a drop of the national and fell asleep. Suddenly someone shouted, "Time for the next race!" The judge's boat was already at the head of the pond, but our friend, hearing the shout, jumped to his feet and ran madly down the wharf and jumped into what he thought was the boat, but there was no boat there. Friends pulled the humiliated fellow from the pond and the race went ahead on schedule without him.

Paddy Flynn

Captain Paddy Flynn from Placentia Bay turned to rum-running during Prohibition to support his family. Flynn quickly adapted to his new profession and became very skillful in avoiding customs officials. When a customs boat was patrolling the area, Flynn would take his relatively small schooner into a shallow cove and wait for the customs boat to move up the coast.

One of his evasion techniques was to frequently change the paint colour on his boat. Flynn told friends, "Those customs guys were smart fellas. They'd stay up nights figuring ways to catch us." Flynn, and those he associated with, came up with a strategy to outwit the "customs fellas." Contacts were needed while enroute to pick up and deliver contraband liquor from St. Pierre, and because of this Flynn came up with a password. Upon arriving at a cove, where an associated waited, he would row ashore at a predetermined time of night. "When n'ar shore I'd slew 'er 'round and sheeve 'er stern first," Captain Flynn recalled. By this he meant coming ashore stern first.

In this type of business there was always the fear of competing rum-runners raiding and stealing your cargo. Captain Paddy's plan for such a surprise was to sit in the stern of his dory armed with a six-foot-long piece of wood from a broken oar, "Me nightstick," as Paddy referred to it.

On one occasion, after following his own rules and placing himself in position to pass on a supply of contraband rum, Paddy heard water splashing which he assessed as the waves rolling in on the nearby sandy beach. He gave the password and waited for a reply. None was forthcoming.

The next step for Paddy was to firmly seize his night stick and wait silently. As swift as a bolt of lightning, out of nowhere, four hands grabbed the stern of the dory. Just as speedily, Paddy swept into action and hammered repeatedly at the exposed hands of his uninvited guests. The victims agonizing roars were followed by roars of "Pull you devils!" by Paddy as he moved out into deep water. His attackers, with smashed hands and broken fingers, were forced to let go leaving Captain Flynn to escape.

It wasn't too long after this, that Captain Flynn was forced to draw from his bag of tricks to outsmart the customs boat. Flynn and associates had developed a one numeral code (two)

130

which covered several situations. This code was explained by historian P.J. Wakeham:

> Two was their code. Two days were allowed for fog. Two days for a storm and if they were supposed to land a part of their cargo at a place and were prevented from doing so, two ports further up the coast would be the landing area, depending on which or what port the purchaser designated.[5]

Throughout these rum-running adventures, the crews were never short of rum, and while avoiding pursuing customs boats hid out in coves where they had plenty of time to sleep, rest and eat.

Another trick Captain Flynn used, was to deliver cargoes of rum at night, which he then buried in the sand. The following day, Flynn would be back in Placentia, or over on St. Pierre, and the customer would retrieve his delivery from the sand. In some cases, this method was used to move cargoes from cove to cove when it seemed that customs were on to them.

The best evasive tactic created by Captain Paddy Flynn was his use of priests clothing, which he carried along on his rum-running escapades and held in reserve until needed. He confided to his closest friends that he was not proud of doing this but resorted to using it only when no other solution was possible.

Such an occasion occurred when the custom's cutter the *Shulamite* was blocking his departure from a cove behind Lawn Islands, which he frequently used when adhering to the smuggler's code, two. The two days hidden to avoid bad weather had expired, the skies were clear and winds ideal to sail. However, he got a glimpse of the *Shulamite* in a position offshore and felt certain the presence of his schooner had been noticed.

5 Wakeham, P.J. *Decks Awash.* 1973.

Captain Flynn was carrying a good supply of contraband to one of his best customers. He felt he could wait no longer. He turned to a mate and said, "God forgive me, I don't want to do this but it got to be done." After consuming a stiff drink of rum he went below deck, after telling the crew to sail towards St. Pierre full speed ahead.

With the schooner now heading towards the cutter, the crew worried. The captain had not come up. Up to this time, the crew was unaware of their captain's plan. At the appropriate time the captain appeared on deck, but now dressed as a Catholic priest.

"Steer her close to the *Shulamite* so this clergyman can wave a friendly greeting to the captain and crew of the cutter," he told the helmsman. Flynn recalled that his crew crossed their fingers and prayed as we crossed paths, waving to the customs officials. "By God it worked," Flynn recalled.

World War II Military Secret and Prohibition

An amusing incident, one of many relating to Prohibition, occurred in the summer of 1945 after the invasion of Normandy, while troops were still advancing across France.

Dr. Noel Murphy, a former leader of the Progressive Conservative Party of Newfoundland and Labrador, was serving with the 125 Newfoundland Squadron of the Royal Air Force.

This was a critical period in the war with heavy demands being placed on the troops. The English coastal area was covered with troops and massive amounts of military equipment were being prepared to cross the Channel to bring an end to the war. Needless to say, this area became a prime target of the Luftwaffe, especially at night.

Dr. Murphy recalled,

I was the medical officer for the squadron, responsible for their health, but I also served as a medical officer for any airfield where we were stationed, backing up the squadron medical officer.[9] Shortly after I joined the squadron, I was informed by the Adjutant that I had been appointed as welfare officer for the unit. I had no idea what this entailed, but learned as time went by that many things were thrown to me to deal with. Chief amongst them were many personal matters involving our personnel and their families.

Dr. Murphy explained:

A large percentage of the ground crews were Newfoundlanders, some of whom had been overseas for several years, and had not been able to visit their homes and families for that period. In case of severe hardship at home it might be possible sometimes, to arrange a discharge from the service–but it was rare. In those cases I would have to make a very good case for the applicant which then went to higher levels for consideration.

A case which Dr. Murphy never forgot occurred when one of the soldiers came to him with a matter of deep personal urgency, which did not involve sickness.

"What can I do for you?" Murphy asked.

"I have to go home, and I want you to arrange it as quickly as possible," he replied.

"Well, you will have to give me a good reason."

"I'm sorry, sir, I can't tell you. You will have to take my word for it. It is vitally important that I get home as soon as possible."

9 *Downhomer Magazine*, St. John's, NL. Feature by Dr. Noel Murphy, 1986. p125

Dr. Murphy explained to him that it was not a question of whether he believed him or not, but he had to go to higher levels and they would demand a justifiable reason for the request.

"Well, sir, I can't tell you. You will just have to take my word for it."

"Then I'm sorry," replied Murphy.

At this point, the conversation abruptly ended and the soldier in frustration walked out. Early the next day, the soldier was back in Murphy's office pleading, "Please, just take my word for it, it's terribly important and very urgent that I get home as quickly as possible."

Once more, Murphy insisted that although he was willing to help, without an explanation to support the request there was not a thing he could do. It was not the answer the soldier was hoping for. Disturbed by his failure to convince the doctor, he got up and without any comment left the office.

The soldier was growing more and more aggravated by his failure to get the approval he needed, but the matter was of prime importance to him. So much so, that he returned to Murphy's office three more times over the following days. His story remained the same each time.

Then he came back displaying much caution as he looked around the waiting area to assure nobody would be listening to the conversation he was about to engage in with the doctor. He was in a sweat when he pulled up a chair next to the doctor's desk and in a low voice said, "If I tell you my reason for wanting to get home will you keep it a secret?"

"I will still have to make your case to my superiors," Murphy replied.

The soldier pondered the situation and after some hesitation said, "OK, I will tell you, but keep it to yourself!"

He then revealed his secret:

Before the war my father and I had a good business going. We live at the bottom of the Burin Peninsula and we used to take our boat over to St. Pierre every so often and get a load of booze, mostly rum, which we brought back and sold. When I left to join up, my father kept the business going by himself. I got a letter last week telling me that he had a run in with the customs officers while still at sea. Some shots were fired and he was arrested. He is now in jail, and I have got to get home as quickly as possible to keep the business going! Now do you understand how important it is, and why we have to keep it secret?[10]

In the end, the final decision was the war effort needed this man far more than the rum-running service in Newfoundland. Dr. Murphy when telling his story would add, "I'm not sure that he understood my reasoning, but whenever I have a drink of rum, I toast him."

A Prohibition Story that Beats all Others!

In 1928, *The Veteran*, a magazine distributed to World War I veterans throughout Newfoundland, published a humorous Prohibition story about a soccer team from the Burin area that ingeniously used a planned soccer game in St. Pierre to outsmart customs and smuggle contraband liquor into Burin. The author A.G. King told readers, "Numerous and varied are the stories which have been told concerning Prohibition, but I think that the following beats them all."
King wrote:

In a certain fishing settlement on the South Coast in 1920 the young male population organized a football [soccer] club and formed a team of which they felt

10 Ibid

very proud. After a few practice matches the prowess of the team was considered unbeatable and enthusiasm was very high. Consequently its supporters began to look around for opponents to conquer.

There was at the time a very strong soccer team at St. Pierre, and negotiations were entered into to hold a series of matches. The local team and its supporters prepared to visit St. Pierre and decided to cross over in two large motor trap skiffs.

Now there was a customs officer living in the settlement who had a fast motor boat which he used in carrying out his duties of protecting the customs. This wise official, anxious to prevent smuggling from St. Pierre by the soccer team and no doubt wishing to witness the matches, decided on crossing to St. Pierre in his own boat, and so keep an eye on the boys and therefore deter them from loading their boats with rum and tobacco.

Everything went well, three very pleasant days were spent on the island and the customs official was satisfied that no smuggling had taken place as he had the teams boats carefully watched.

On the morning of the fourth day the team decided to return. They therefore embarked and started home accompanied by the customs' boat. As the customs boat was much speedier than the trap skiffs, the customs official decided to go ahead and land at the settlement moor his own boat and then visit the pier where the team was to disembark and examine their boats and luggage as an extra precaution against smuggling. This he did and nothing of a dutiable nature was found. No doubt, he was now quite proud of himself and confident he had outfoxed the team.

That same night, however, there was considerable jollification and plenty of intoxication in the settlement.

In fact, he noticed that most of the men seemed to be drunk. The customs officer was considerably surprised and puzzled, but his surprise was not to be compared with his chagrin and amazement when later he discovered the truth. He learned that whilst he was carefully watching the team's trap skiffs at St. Pierre, the members of the team purchased their stocks and loaded it all onboard his customs boat. After arriving home they unloaded it from the customs boat at the same time the officer was examining their trap skiffs.

It is said that some of the football team were grateful enough afterwards to thank the customs officer for bringing them their rum from St. Pierre.

The Good Luck Captain

Prohibition in the United States and Canada offered an opportunity, although an illegal one, for Newfoundland fishermen to make extra money during hard financial times. It is not surprising then to learn that many fishermen availed of the new source of revenue by turning to rum-running. One such crew was made up of five brothers from Conception Bay, all of whom was of good moral character and did not give any thought to bootlegging or rum-running.

However, they never considered what they would do if they were in a situation where they could easily rip-off professional rum-runners, and get away with it. Unexpectedly, they walked right into a set of circumstances which presented them with just such an opportunity. It was too good to pass up, and they didn't.

As in most cases, the names of rum-runners and bootleggers during the Prohibition years generally only survived if they were arrested, made the news, or revealed their secrets. In the case of these five brothers, their tale became a well-known anecdote of the era and is remembered simply as a "Captain Good Luck Adventure."

While fishing near Petty Harbour one day, their schooner ran short of fresh water and pulled into a small cove not far from the community. It was while scouring the area for a good source of drinking water that the captain's good luck began. Looking southward, he noticed a large white canvas covering something partially hidden by some bushes.

Before going to take a look, his eyes scanned the entire area to see if there was any other life nearby. Satisfied he was alone, Captain Good Luck made his way to the object and began to uncover it. This was a more difficult job than he had anticipated because the canvas had been secured with rope. He struggled to open it, and when it was partially revealed he couldn't believe his eyes.

"There was a bloody fortune in rum, brandy, whiskey, gin, cigarettes and fine cigars," he later told friends.

This was a turning point in the lives of the five fishermen as they pondered the possibilities of turning their discovery into a fat profit. The captain rationalized what they were about to do. He told his brothers:

Look here, this is all contraband cargo, smuggled here from St. Pierre from only God knows where. This belongs to crooks so what's the harm in stealing it from them and making some money for ourselves. The Good Lord knows we can use it.

The others readily agreed. The captain was fortunate to have a good schooner with a new engine along with canvas sails and plenty of storage room. Once the contraband was aboard, each brother took two bottles of rum for personal consumption.

The captain ordered a stop to his fishing operation and set sail for his home port in Conception Bay. Although he had not considered either rum-running or bootlegging, he was now the manager of a small operation which would, in the succeeding months, rob contraband liquor from rum-runners and bootleggers through a contact living in St. John's.

After negotiating a deal with the St. John's businessman, the captain needed a method to smuggle the supplies without being detected. During a sleepless night trying to work out a scheme, he came up with a truly creative idea. In his home community barrels were plentiful. Every kind of food, fish and vegetable were stored in these barrels. He explained to his brothers, "We will ship the contraband in barrels with the other deliveries going to St. John's." It worked. But this was not the end of this captain's good luck.

While doing business in St. John's, the captain stayed at a downtown hotel. While in the bathroom one night, he overheard a conversation between two men. They spoke in low tones, but not so low that Captain Good Luck could not hear them. In their conversation, they discussed the pending arrival of a schooner loaded with contraband liquor and tobacco to Conception Bay. They mentioned the time and place where they would meet with the schooner and that they would use several motor skiffs to take the illegal cargo ashore. He even overheard their password.

The captain returned home next day and called a meeting with his brothers. He also increased their little operation to include several other relatives. Captain Good Luck's good fortune was on a roll. He told them, "This will be an easy job. All we need to do is to go out farther than the point they were going to meet the others, I'll pass meself of as their customer and tell them there was a change of plans for security reasons and I was sent out the bay further then originally intended."

It was a bold tactic, but the captain was a real charmer and up to the challenge. After stopping the rum-runners and giving them the password, he had no trouble convincing them of the change. He chuckled to himself as the rum-running crew swept into operation to unload a fortune in contraband onto his schooner. He accepted a drink of rum from the rum-runners, then waved farewell as he sailed into moonlit Conception Bay. He was not called Captain Good Luck for nothing. As his schooner moved away, clouds began blanketing the moon.

About two months later he had developed a string of customers along Conception Bay who brought in their own boats to pick up their purchases of contraband liquor.

Several days later, the victimized schooner entered the port where its captain had been instructed to take her, but she was in for another surprise. After unknowingly selling contraband rum to an undercover police officer, a team of police officers boarded the vessel, seized it and arrested the captain. The remaining cargo still on board was confiscated and became property of the Newfoundland government.

The schooner was owned by a prominent St. John's merchant who had to pay a hefty fine to have his vessel returned to him. Captain Good Luck had no remorse for his actions. He explained:

> The way I looked upon it was, those people were very wealthy and they were out to beat the law by hook or by crook and they were willing to take a chance on smuggling to further increase their riches. The fishery hadn't been good with us all year, and we have large families, so I looked upon the episode as a real windfall. We lived high on the hog that winter.[6]

Sailors Robbed the Coast Guard

A rum-runner on its routine run to deliver its contraband cargo along Rum Row encountered the unexpected — a fire. A cutter from New York, on its routine sweep of the area, happened along, and succeeded in, putting out the fire thereby

6 P.J. Wakeham. *New-Land Magazine.* Spring 1973, Vol . 23.

saving the crew and its cargo. The rum-runner was towed to New York and tied up at the wharf. The cargo of rum was unloaded and stored in an open shed near the wharf. This was an area frequented by sailors going to and from their ships. Before long, the cargo of liquor began dwindling. The liquor was smuggled inside the jackets and shirts of sailors. News of the theft leaked and caused quite a scandal and much discomfort in Coast Guard circles.

Coast Guard and customs officials were always on guard against rum-runners, who after being caught would make false charges against them, accusing the officials of stealing sextants, charts, time pieces and even personal property from their vessels. The hoods made sure such information was leaked to the press, who quite often were having their palms greased. The law regarding seizure required that the vessel, tackle, apparel and furniture be taken into custody at the time of the seizure.

To offset this sort of reprisal, the U.S. attorney would seek a change of venue to a federal court, over which the local court had no jurisdiction. These cases rarely made it to trial because the feds did not pursue them. Neither did the complaints who were satisfied that the smear had gotten news coverage.

Bribed the Law

In cases where charges were laid, much hard work went into the preparation for trial. Apprehending the rum-running vessel was just the start of the Coast Guards work. Evidence had to be gathered, recorded in detail and preserved. Lawyers representing the rum-runners or gang members involved showed little regard for truth or justice.

Malcolm Willoughby, a senior officer with the U.S. Coast Guard and later an historian and author observed, "The unpopularity of Prohibition generally and the sympathy evidenced by the public and sometimes by the courts for those engaged in its circumvention were discouraging."

The bribes not only included law enforcers but also court judges. Willoughby pointed out, "One federal judge whose district included Connecticut was so biased that, regardless of the completeness and nature of evidence, conviction was virtually impossible." Things were so bad in the Connecticut jurisdiction, that the U.S. Coast Guard issued instructions that seized vessels were not to be brought into that jurisdiction if any alternate choice was available. The Connecticut coastline was a large part of Rum Row, frequented by the Newfoundland rum-running Navy.[7]

When Coast Guard officers noted a new fishing boat heading towards New York harbour with a suspicious looking crew, they ordered its captain to stop. The officers sent aboard found it was carrying a load of fish. A search from stem to stern was carried out, but could not find any trace of liquor. The Coast Guard captain remained highly suspicious. He later told reporters, "I just had this strong gut feeling that things were not right so I escorted the ship into New York port for a closer look."

Throughout this process, the fishing captain loudly protested their action and threatened to sue for damages resulting from spoiled fish. This caused the officals to be concerned until the captain noted that the hold appeared to be rather shallow for a fishing schooner. A further investigation, during which a line was passed under the keel from port to starboard, revealed a discrepancy between the depth of the hold and the draft of the boat.

The Coast Guard captain spared no effort in uncovering the deception. His crew were ordered to burst through the concrete in the bilges, while officers bored through wooden planking into a hidden compartment below, which was filled with crates of liquor. The gangsters had gone through the

7 Several cases involving Newfoundland rum-runners charged in American courts are told elsewhere in this book.

expense of designing and constructing a false bottom in this rum-running vessel. Armed with this knowledge the Coast Guard uncovered others.[8] These practices were detected by comparing the original measurements of registered documents with the measurements detected during investigation.

All day long, liquor was coming and going from the warehouses in St. Pierre and Newfoundland. Often, the Coast Guard vessels would watch this activity while themselves loading up with supplies and fuel. At this point it was all legal. Only when it was being delivered along Rum Row, the New Jersey to Boston coast, did the Coast Guard sweep in to intercept the smugglers. Prohibition in the United States came to an end in 1933.

Prohibition Songs

In the era prior to Prohibition, the sale of liquor in taverns was handled much differently than today. Drinks ordered inside a tavern were not sold by the glass. The customer had to order a bottle, which would be laid in front of the customer along with a glass or two.

A $1.20 would get you a bottle of Scotch whisky, thirty cents for a bottle of the best rum. Fifteen cents was the cost of an imported beer, and local beer sold for ten cents. Bars charged twenty cents per drink for spirits, which included the mixer but the bottle was given to the customer to pour himself.[1]

During this time, the police attempted to reduce the number of drunks brought into court each day, on various charges stemming from intoxication, by circulating what became known as the drunk list among the liquor outlets throughout St. John's. All those who appeared in court on liquor-related charges were placed on the list, and a copy was given to each liquor store. In response, Jimmy Murphy, who

1 "The Big Drought" - (Sic) Phillip, *Newfoundland Lifestyle Magazine*
8 Robinson, George. *It Came by the Boatload.*

was a partner in writing with the famous "Bard of Prescott Street," Johnny Burke, penned the song called:

"On The List"

Oh! Danny, dear, I heard the "cops"
On Yesterday they dropped
A notice to all rum-shops
For to say our drinks are stopped.
I'm told, my wife, and yours also,
To do so, did insist,
We dare not to the "gin mill" go,
For now we're on the list.

Chorus
No more the police shall "run us in,"
With a bracelet on each wrist.
We're done of "loading to the chin,"
For now we're on the list.

No more we'll stagger home at night,
To kick and cuff and swear.
Our little children from our sight,
And to tear our poor wife's hair.
The "pleasures" that they did endure,
They never will be missed,
Oh! Danny, dear, they have found the cure–
For now, we're on the list.

Oh! Danny, dear, I do declare,
'Tis the best thing that could be,
To keep us from going "on the beer,"
For 'twould ruin both you and me.

Too long unto the gin-mill, Dan,
We brought our hard-earned grist,
So, cheer up, Dan, shake hands, "old man,"
For now, we're on the list.

Liquor Book

When Prohibition ended, the only outlets licensed to sell alcohol were those owned and operated by the Newfoundland government.[3] With this practice, several new words entered the Newfoundland glossary: controller and liquor book. Newfoundlanders, well into the first decades of Confederation, referred to liquor stores as the controllers or the Bond store, and sang the famous "Liquor Book Song" written by Johnny Jones of Pleasant Street. Possession of a liquor book enabled the owner to purchase one bottle of liquor weekly. This was later increased to two bottles. The customer was required to present his liquor book to the clerk at the controllers who would record the purchase as long as it was within the limit.

Bootleggers found a way to get around this restriction. Friends, relatives and regular customers were recruited to purchase liquor for them by using their individual liquor books in cases where they couldn't afford the price themselves or were not drinkers.

The owner of a permit could write a note allowing the bearer of the permit to pick up his quota of liquor. It wasn't uncommon to stand in a line-up at the controllers during Christmas, while a customer with an armful of liquor books put in his orders.

Johnny Jones of Pleasant Street, St. John's, was famous throughout most of Newfoundland in the 1940s and 1950s for his song sheets related to the issues of the day. His most memorable song was "The Liquor Book Song"— tune "Kelligrews Soiree". It was recorded decades later by the

3 Fitzgerald, Jack. *Newfoundland's Era of Corruption.* Creative Publishers. 2013

popular Dick Nolan, and, incorrectly, one writer noted that Nolan had written it. Part of the song follows:

"The Liquor Book Song"

After workin' all the live long year there finally comes a day
my two weeks summer holidays and a trip around the bay
and kickin' off my overalls I marched out in my glee
determined to get a bottle of screech to take along with me.

There were people there from everywhere
Grand Falls and Corner Brook
from Joe Batt's Arm and Billy's farm all waitin'
for their book.

There were young men with curly hair and old men
with bald heads
and pretty little maidens, old maids with wooden legs
old men with whiskers on their chin who gave
an awful look
and there whiskers they grew longer as they waited
for their book.

Americans Quench Thirst

During Prohibition many Americans crossed the border into Canada, where in several provinces they were free to purchase and drink as much liquor as they wanted. An unidentified writer penned some verses summing up the high regard they held for Canadian-manufactured liquor. These were sung to the tune of "Sing a Song of Sixpence." The song gained widespread popularity, and even reached the ears of

King George V of England who was visibly amused by it. The verses read:

> Four and twenty Yankees,
> Feeling mighty dry,
> Took a trip to Canada
> And brought a case of rye.
>
> When the case was opened
> The Yanks began to sing
> "To hell with the President,
> God save the King."[4]

4 Sinclair, Andrew. *Prohibition: The Era of Excesses*. Little, Brown and Company. Pp 335.

Police officials assuring that barrels of beer taken from the mob went down the sewer. Library of Congress.

A rum-running fishing vessel captured by customs officials. PANL

Al Capone with hat in hand.
Photo courtesy of Kay Coady

Prime Minister Sir Richard
Squires was described by Hollis
Walker, who headed Royal
Commission on corruption in the
Newfoundland government, as
the country's biggest bootlegger.
PANL

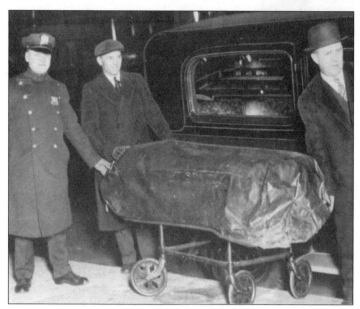

Legs Diamond, a prominent New York mobster was shot down in his apartment house shortly after repaying money stolen from the mob. According
to those who knew him at the time, he raised his payment while hiding out
in St. John's. Photo courtesy of The Maritimes, U.S. National Archives

Sir Edward Morris (seated, third from left) joins officers of the
Newfoundland Regiment in presenting a caribou head to the burgh of Ayr,
Scotland. Lady Morris is seated, centre. PANL

Prime Minister
Fredrik Alderice
1932-1934
PANL

L-R: Bill Cruikshank, his uncle
Captain Ed Dicks. Bill's death
in Halifax was a suspected
murder, carried out by
gangsters in the trade
George Anderson.

A PORTION OF THE SAINT PIERRE WHARF CIRCA 1924.

These pictures are uncommon. Photography was discouraged, as the French government was stoutly denying that the Islands were involved in smuggling to the United States.

Case goods (whiskey, gin, etc.) were often unpacked on the wharf and placed in burlap bags for ease of transport. These are visible in the background. Other boxes are unopened. There are numerous kegs, some containing French West Indian rum (no Demerara rum was allowed on the Islands), and others containing bulk whiskey.

Frecker & Steer were brothers-in-law who owned the store in the background, supplying the needs of schooners and their crews. They were not primarily liquor dealers.

Courtesy: Musée du Nouveau Monde, La Rochelle.

The Freckers Distillery, St. Pierre. PANL

American Coast Guard cutter delivers a cargo of contraband liquor into New York harbour, captured from rum-runners along Rum Row.
U.S. Coast Guard

The luxurious Dalvay By The Sea was purchased and owned by Newfoundland rum-runner of Prohibition, Captain Edward Dicks. He purchased it from Alexander MacDonald of the Standard Oil Company, who had it built in 1896. After registering the sale in his wife's name, he spent a large amount of money converting it into a splendid summer hotel.
Geoff Robinson

The *Nellie J. Banks* off the North Shore in the late 1930s.
Courtesy of the R.C.M.P

The *Nellie J. Banks*, Newfoundland-owned and with a Newfoundland crew made Prohibition history by sparking the R.C.M.P. investigation that shocked North America by exposing an extensive conspiracy in the rum-running rackets. St. Pierre honoured the little boat with a post card and stamp.
Geoff Robinson

This photograph shows one of the phoney ten dollar bills used to swindle a top Prohibition bootlegger and rum-runner. Public Archives of Canada

155

Epilogue

Some Newfoundlanders mentioned in this book earned some recognition in the years after Prohibition. Joseph R. Smallwood was the journalist travelling on the Royal Navy vessel, which landed troops on an island in Green Bay to break up a large moonshine operation. While still in his twenties, Smallwood was a political advisor to Sir Richard Squires, and became a household name throughout Newfoundland through the broadcast of his radio program *The Barrelman*.

Joseph Smallwood, prodigious researcher and writer, by the time the referendum on Confederation was called by Britain, was the best informed Newfoundlander on the Canadian political system and its social programs. He led the Confederates to success in 1948 and became Newfoundland's first premier in 1949.

Les Curtis, a partner with Sir Richard Squires' law firm became a member of the first Newfoundland cabinet under its new premier.

John McEvoy, who was a lawyer for many rum-runners, became prominent in the Confederate party and connived behind the scenes to persuade his friends in Ottawa to appoint him as the first premier.

Tom Power, of Haggerty Street, St. John's, who got close to Capone while working on the ship the gangster leased for two year periods, became active in the Longshore Fishermen's Protective Union in St. John's, but rarely talked about his experience. The picture of him, wearing Capone's suit is still in possession of the Power family.

Henri Morez, a Capone contact on St. Pierre confided his involvement to St. Pierre author and historian, J.P Andrieux. His knowledge of Capone and Prohibition was invaluable to Andrieux and to a series of authors who have since researched Capone.

Costiglia was a mob member in New York who played a role in the bootlegging and rum-running operations. He later took over the mafia, as it became known, and changed his name to Frank Costello. The FBI caught up with him in 1958.

Nick Markis, who shot Gustav Carlos to death in a St. Pierre bar, is believed to have escaped to the United States, changed his identity and was never found. However, he was tried and convicted in absentia on St. Pierre on March 18, 1821. His sentence was life imprisonment.

The Bronfman brothers were not convicted of any crime, and went on to develop one Canada's most successful breweries.

A number of people who were registered as Newfoundland-born and served on the mob-owned fleet of eighty-one could not be traced.

As for me, I was faced with a near death crisis while still writing this book, however, it was not mob related! Thanks to the expert team of doctors and nurses at St. Claire's Hospital, I survived and was able to complete *Rum-runners and Mobsters: Prohibition's 100th Anniversary in Newfoundland*...many thanks to Dr. Gardiner!

Acknowledgements

I acknowledge with sincere gratitude, the assistance and support given to me in my effort to bring *Rum-runners and Mobsters: Prohibition's 100th Anniversary in Newfoundland* to publication, the following people: Bob Rumsey, Don Morgan, Maurice Fitzgerald Photography, Donna Francis and Pam Dooley. I am also grateful to the staffs of: the QEII Library, Memorial University's Centre for Newfoundland Studies, the City of St. John's Archives, the A.C Hunter Library, Newfoundland Collection and the Provincial Archives of Newfoundland and Labrador.

Bibliography

Reports and Journals
The Royal Commission on the Liquor Traffic, The Facts of the Case. By F. S. Spence, Secretary, The Dominion Alliance for the total suppression of the Liquor Traffic.

"Rum running in the good old days," *Newfoundland Lifestyles*, 1986, John Calver,Vol. 4(1) pp 38,39. And Henri Moraze, St. Pierre and Mcquelon, 1918-1933.

"Prohibition and St. Pierre," *Newfoundland Quarterly*, Spring 1984, Vol. 79(4), pp 31,32. Andrieux, Jean-Pierre, "Prohibition and Politics," *Newfoundland Herald*, Ab Stockwood, August 2, 1986, Vol. 41 (31)

Colonial Commerce, February 28, 1917, Vol. 26.(3) pp17-22. "Prohibition, humour and sport" Anderson, John. *Decks Awash*, Contraband, January-February 1984, Vol. 13(1), pp 56-57

"The Prohibition Racket -1898-1924," *Newscene*, January 23, 1970, p8, Rev E. Hunt.

"A Prohibition Story" (1920 incident), *Veteran Magazine*, December 1928, Vol 7(4), p82. Prohibition Humour, *Veteran Magazine*, December 1921, Vol 1(1) pp44-46, King, A.G.

"The Big Drought, Prohibition- St. John's Woman," November 1963, pp17-19. [Sic] Phillips

"A unique industry maybe killed by recent Prohibition Act," H.F. Shortis, (Re-opening of port wine in Newfoundland Shortis Journal Vol 2(398) p2

Screech and Prohibition -1640-1924, Moakler, Leo.

"Wartime Top Secret" - 1942 incident of Newfoundland RAF ground crewman needing discharge. *Downhomer*, January, 1999, Vol.11(8) p125, Murphy, Dr. Noel F.

"The Sinking of the I'm Alone," Thorne, Robert G. , *Downhomer*, October 2001, Vol. 14 (5)

"Wakeham, P. J., Mr. "B"s rum running episodes," *New-Land Magazine*, Spring 1973, Col 23. *Contraband Cargo, A True experience as told by J.J. Flynn, Newfoundland Story, Christmas 1947, Vol 2 (1) .Contraband Cargo, A true experience as told by J.J. Flynn- Rumrunning Incident.*

"The Rum-running incident," *Atlantic Insight*, February 1983, Vol 5 (2) P47 St. Pierre and Miquelon, Bonnie Woodward.

Books
Andrieux, Jean Pierre, *Prohibition and St. Pierre*,W. F. Rannie, Lincoln, Ont. 1983. *Over the Side: Stories from a rumrunner's files from Prohibition days in Atlantic Canada and Newfoundland*, W. F. Rannie, Beamsbille, Ontario, 1984

Baker, Melvin, 1921 *report of the Commission on the Prohibition Plebiscite Act*, Newfoundland and Labrador Studies, Fall 2012, Vo;/ 27 (2) pp 267-279

Coffey, Thomas M. , *The Long Thirst, Prohibition in America: 1920-1933*, W.W. Norton & Company, New York,1975

Hunter, Mark C., *Changing the flag: The cloak of Newfoundland Registry for American rum-running, 1924-1934.* Pp 41-69

Hunt, C.W. , *Whisky and Ice, The Saga of Ben Kerr, Canada's Most Daring Rumrunner*, Dundurn Press, Toronto and Oxford. 1995

Mapper, Marc, *Prohibition Gangsters*, Rutgers University Press, New Brunswick, New Jersey and London 2013— for pics contact Rutgers University Press, 106 Somerset Street, New Brunswick, New Jersey, 08901

Noel, S.J.R., *Politics in Newfoundland*, University of Toronto Press, 1971, p131,132,133.

Robinson, George and Dorothy, *It Came by the Boatload*, Alfa Graphics, PEI, 1985. T*he Nellie J. Banks, the life history of a Nova Scotian Schooner with a Newfoundland crew that helped Prince Edward Islanders cope with prohibition.,* self-published, Tyne Valley, PEI 1970

Sinclair, Andrew, *An All Monthly Press Book*, Little, Brown and Company, Boston & Toronto-1962

Smallwood, Joseph R., *Encyclopedia of Newfoundland and Labrador, Vol. One*, Newfoundland Book Publishers (1967) Limited.

Willoughby, Malcolm, *Rum War at Sea*, US Government Printing Office, 1964.

Personal Interviews
Kay Coady, in-law of Tom Power who was a crewman
on the boat leased by Capone. James Martin, St. John's,
a former Vice-President of LSPU. Also gathered related
information from LSPU members who recalled Legs
Diamonds waterfront activities in St. John's during
Prohibition. Sgt. William Bennett, RCA, who was a font
of information about old St. John's.

Also Available

Jack Fitzgerald's Treasury of Newfoundland Stores, Volume II: Amazing and Strange
Jack Fitzgerald's Treasury of Newfoundland Stories, Volume I: True Crime and Adventure
Peculiar Facts and Tales of Newfoundland
Newfoundland's Era of Corruption: Responsible Government, 1855-1934
1949: The Twilight Before the Dawn
The Spring Rice Document
Battlefront Newfoundland
Crimes that Shocked Newfoundland
The Jack Ford Story: Newfoundland POW in Nagasaki
Legacy of Laughter
Remarkable Stories of Newfoundland
Treasure Island Revisited: A True Newfoundland Adventure Story
Ten Steps to the Gallows: True Stories of Newfoundland and Labrador
Newfoundland Adventures: In Air, On Land, At Sea
Where Angels Fear to Tread
Another Time, Another Place
Amazing Newfoundland Stories
The Hangman is Never Late
Untold Stories of Newfoundland
Beyond the Grave
Beyond Belief
Strange but True Newfoundland Stories
Jack Fitzgerald's Notebook
Ghosts and Oddities
Stroke of Champions
Up the Pond
A Day at the Races: The Story of the St. John's Regatta
Newfoundland Disasters
Rogues and Branding Irons
Convicted
Too Many Parties, Too Many Pals
Incredible Stories of Newfoundland
Newfoundland Fireside Stories

Ask your favourite bookstore or order directly from the publisher.

Creative Book Publishing
36 Austin Street St. John's, Newfoundland A1B 3T7

Tel: (709)-748-0813 • Fax: (709) 579-6511
E-mail: nl.books@transcontinental.ca • www.creativebookpublishing.ca